The shout

The Ascension of our Lord Jesus Christ and His continuing work today

Derek Prime

DayOne

© Derek Prime 1999
First printed 1999

Scripture quotations are from The New King James Version.
Copyright © 1990, 1985, 1983 by Thomas Nelson, Inc.

British Library Cataloguing in Publication Data available
ISBN 0 902548 90 5

Published by Day One Publications
3 Epsom Business Park, Kiln Lane, Epsom, Surrey KT17 1JF.
01372 728 300 FAX 01372 722 400
e-mail address: sales@dayone.co.uk
web site: www.dayone.co.uk

Designed by Steve Devane and printed by Clifford Frost Ltd, Wimbledon SW19 2SE

Contents

O f all I have written, this book is the one I have most wanted to write and the one I have found the most daunting. Both statements require some explanation. I have wanted to explore the subject ever since I realised that our Lord Jesus Christ's Ascension and continuing work (often called His *session* because He sits at God's right hand) are among the most neglected aspects of His ministry. Any neglect of them is detrimental to the Church's spiritual health and outlook.

The desire to explore this topic increased as I detected in the Old Testament the significance of *the shout of a King* in the experience of the people of Israel. They possessed this benefit without possessing at the time any human sovereign. While it was obvious to all observing nations that Israel had no visible King, it was nevertheless possible for God's people to know *the shout of a King* among them. God Himself was their King! When they appreciated this truth and lived accordingly, they were spiritually healthy and able to serve Him. When they took their eyes off their King, they soon blundered and failed. They then brought both dishonour to God and disaster to themselves.

To consider the significance of the Ascension and continuing work of our Lord Jesus Christ focuses attention on our invisible King. Only as we recognise Him as our glorious Sovereign and fix our eyes on Him, may we serve Him effectively in the world.

The daunting aspect of the subject is its vastness and, in some respects at least, its unexplored nature. My fear has been that I might not deal with it adequately, and thus fail the One whose unique and glorious work this book attempts to explore. Nevertheless, it is better to stutter than to be dumb! I can echo the words of the writer of the wedding song of Psalm 45:1: 'My heart is overflowing with a good theme; I recite my composition concerning the King.'

Justification for the study

A number of grounds underline the importance of studying our Lord Jesus Christ's Ascension and continuing work for His Church. We begin with the basic truth that 'The works of the LORD are great, Studied by all who have pleasure in them' (Psalm 111:2). Those words greet all who enter the Cavendish Laboratory in the University of Cambridge, famous for its scientific discoveries. Wonderful and glorious as God's work of creation is, and worthy of scientific investigation, more wonderful still is His mighty work of redemption.

First, the Ascension was as much an act of God's power as the Resurrection (Ephesians 1:19-21). The work the Lord Jesus currently pursues is one He alone can do as the divine Saviour and High Priest of His people. All God's works are worthy subjects for meditation. Meditation is like climbing a mountain. It takes effort and time, but it is the only way to capture the unique view of all around from the top. If we do not take time to ponder our Lord Jesus' work, we will fail to appreciate the full consequences of the great things He has done for us. As Andrew Bonar put it, 'Meditation is letting God speak to us until our heart is throbbing.' Delight in God our Saviour is synonymous with delight in His works.

Second, Luke, whose concern in writing his gospel was to report all the evidence of the eye-witnesses of Jesus' ministry, ends his gospel record with the Ascension. He then begins the book of *Acts* with a more detailed description of it. He plainly believed that something dramatically significant happened when our Lord returned to heaven. It drew a dividing line. It closed one book and opened another. Before the Ascension it was the Lord Jesus Christ who proclaimed the message of salvation. Now it was over to His disciples to take up this task. Our Saviour had pursued His Father's will and purpose as He taught, preached and made Himself the servant of others, in the interests of God's kingdom. After the Ascension, Jesus' representatives were to do the same.

The manner in which Luke starts his history of the early Church— *The Acts of the Apostles*—hints at a 'handing over' of responsibility. He begins, 'The former account I made, O Theophilus, of all that Jesus began both to do and teach, until the day in which He was taken up, after He through the Holy Spirit had given commandments to the apostles whom He had chosen' (Acts 1:1,2). Luke shows that what Jesus *began* to do, as written down in his gospel record, the Lord Jesus *continues* to do through His body, the Church. The conclusion of our

Lord's ministry on earth marked the beginning of the Church's activity in co-operation with the Ascended Lord. This may explain why *Acts* ends as it does without telling us what happened to Paul, much as we are curious to know (Acts 28:31). Whatever happens to Jesus Christ's servants, His work continues. What He did in the first century's early decades in the small geographical area of Palestine, He continues to do throughout the whole world by His obedient people.

Third, if we neglect our Saviour's Ascension and continuing work, we may lose sight of His unique and central place in the life of the Church. In recent decades attention has been given to the Person and Work of God the Holy Spirit. I have sometimes found myself uncomfortable at aspects of this concentration. The New Testament teaches that the primary focus of the Spirit is upon the Lord Jesus Christ Himself (for example, John 16:14,15). The Holy Spirit, the Comforter, brings comfort in all our varied experiences principally by encouraging and helping us to look away to the Lord Jesus and to see in Him our all-sufficient Saviour. The Lord Jesus Himself is our hope, and that hope remains vital and alive only as we fix our eyes upon its object. We are to live our lives in the light of *where* our Saviour is, and *what* He does for us now.

Fourth, the convictions of Christians, expressed not least in the creeds of the Church, underline the fundamental importance of the Ascension. 'Every Christian festival condemns the devil, but this one especially,' Chrysostom (c.347-407) pointedly declared.

Ireneaus (c.130-c.200) wrote, 'The Church though scattered throughout the whole world to the ends of the earth, has received from the apostles and their disciples her faith ... in one Christ Jesus ... and His assumption in the flesh into the heavens.'

Later Augustine wrote, 'This is that festival which confirms the grace of all the festivals together, without which the profitableness of every festival would have perished. For unless the Saviour had ascended into heaven, His nativity would have come to nothing ... and His passion would have borne no fruit for us, and His most holy Resurrection would have been useless' (*Sermo. 53.4. Coll. Selec. SS Ecclesiae,* ed. D.A.B. Caillau, p. vii).

Creeds and confessions of faith express the convictions of believers in every generation. *The Apostles' Creed* affirms that following upon His

Resurrection, our Lord Jesus 'ascended into heaven, and is seated at the right hand of the Father.' *The Apostles' Creed* rests upon the Roman baptismal creed of the second century.

The Augsburg Confession of 1530, the official standard of Lutheranism, includes a more detailed statement in its third article. 'The same Christ ... ascended into heaven, and sits on the right hand of God, that He may eternally rule and have dominion over all creatures, that through the Holy Spirit He may sanctify, purify, strengthen, and comfort all who believe in Him, that He may bestow on them life, and every grace and blessing, that He may protect and defend them against the devil and against sin.'

Article IV of the *Thirty-Nine Articles* of the Church of England, affirms, 'Christ did truly rise from death, and took again His body, with flesh, bones and all things appertaining to the perfection of man's nature; wherewith He ascended into heaven, and there sitteth until He return to judge all men at the last day.'

Our purpose

Our subject is first our Lord Jesus Christ's Ascension and its consequences. Two requisites at least are necessary: first, humility and, secondly, care. Humility is imperative in line with the principle established in 1 Corinthians 2:14. 'But the natural man does not receive the things of the Spirit of God, for they are foolishness to him; nor can he know them, because they are spiritually discerned.' The Holy Spirit can enlighten us in our understanding of the Scriptures so that we appreciate all that God has freely given us in His Son's Ascension and continuing work on our behalf. The Spirit alone can give us an understanding that will govern our thinking and lifestyle beyond the mere recitation of a truth contained in a creed or confession of faith. If the death of Jesus determines how I live—and it does—and if the Resurrection of Jesus influences my life—and it does—so should His Ascension.

Second, we need to exercise care as we consider our Lord's continuing work. A few basic and key Scriptures describe it. Sometimes, in a bid to make the significance intelligible and relevant, Christians have tended to speculate about aspects of our Lord's continuing work, where the Bible itself is silent. That is something we want to avoid. Our aim is to establish what we can be completely clear about, avoiding anything that is purely speculative. A good example is when we come to consider the nature of our Lord's present intercession for His Church. There are truths God has chosen not to reveal, and we should not give the status of truth to our hunches or conjectures. As the writer of Proverbs reminds us, 'It is the glory of God to conceal a matter' (Proverbs 25:2). 'He does great things past finding out, Yes, wonders without number' (Job 9:10). God has given us however more than sufficient truth to recognise what is most important, and by which we are to live.

We begin with a significant phrase from the Old Testament to which we shall return at the end of this book—*the shout of a King.*

The shout of a King!

The shout of a King is the assured presence of the Risen and Ascended Lord Jesus that the Church should enjoy as her birthright. What has spurred me most to write this book is the conviction that *the shout of our King* should be a pre-eminent mark of His Church. Tragically, this may not always be the case. We have to think only of the members of the church at Laodicea, described in Revelation 3:15-18. They engaged in all their church activities without recognising that their Lord was 'outside', knocking at their door, wanting to gain entrance (Revelation 3:20).

Both Church history and personal experience show how easily we may lose sight of our Saviour's centrality in the life of His Church. We then stop giving Him the place that He alone deserves. We cease to look for the signs of His presence. Tragic consequences of failure and dishonour to His Name follow. *The shout of a King* should characterise the Church, even as it did God's people in the Old Testament period when they were in a right relationship with Him.

A shout is not necessarily anything exceptional, although it tends to be, even when we hear it on the streets. 'Shout' is an onomatopoeia word. It resembles words like *buzz* or *murmur* that imitate the sounds associated with the objects or actions to which they refer.

Different kinds of shout occur. It may be a shout of joy, or triumph or success. It may be a shout of encouragement when spectators cheer their team at the beginning of a football match or at a crucial point in the game.

The shout of a King is a shout of joy, triumph, success and encouragement rolled into one. The King we have in view is our Risen and Ascended Lord Jesus. This shout is a particular outcome and benefit of His Ascension and His continuing presence with His people.

As already indicated, the Ascension of our Lord Jesus, and His being seated at the right hand of the Father, find a prominent place in the Christian Church's creeds. They represent statements Christians have made throughout the centuries concerning the fundamentals of their faith. *The Apostles Creed* (in place well before 250 AD), *the Nicene Creed* (325 AD) and the so-called *Athanasian Creed* (381-428 AD)—'so-called' because it was written later than Athanasius—give an important place to the Ascension. In the sixteenth century John Calvin wrote in his commentary on *Acts* (on Acts 1:9), 'The Ascension of Christ ... is one of the chief points of our faith.'

In Easter 1996, *The Daily Telegraph* commissioned a Gallup survey on the Christian beliefs of the British population, following an identical survey three years before. The proportion who knew that Good Friday commemorates the crucifixion of Jesus had fallen from 64 to 60 per cent. The proportion familiar with the Ascension had fallen even more, from 37 to 28 per cent. What happens among the public often affects the Church, and it must be true the other way round. If Christian believers do not hold to the elementary truths of the faith, it is not surprising that the world at large does not know about them.

To understand the Ascension of our Lord Jesus Christ is essential to our appreciation of His majesty and glory. When we think about the life of Jesus, we often consider it between two particular boundaries or fixed points: His birth and His death. The Ascension (and all that followed it) reminds us that He *was* before the first fixed point—His human birth— and that His life *continued*, and *continues*, after the other—His death.

We need to reaffirm the Ascension and the significance of Jesus' position at the right hand of the Father as key elements of the Christian faith. Nothing sums up their practical significance more than *the shout of a King*. This phrase intrigued me when I first read it, and I found myself asking what it really meant. Since appreciating something of its significance, it has fostered a desire to know its present reality in the life of the Church. It sums up a truth that both encourages and thrills.

The dilemma of Balaam and Balak

The origin of the phrase is in the Book of Numbers. A strange character called Balaam declared of Israel, God's people, 'The LORD his God is with him, and *the shout of a King* is among them' (Numbers 23:21). As often happens in the Old Testament, we have here an example of parallelism, where one statement explains what immediately precedes or follows it. *The Lord their God being conspicuously with them* was identical to *the shout of a King* being among them. For us *the shout of a King* is *our Lord Jesus Christ's promised presence with us*, in discernible and tangible ways.

Let us go in our imagination to a hill in the Middle East where Balak, a king, and Balaam, a dubious prophet, were looking down on Israelite encampments. The period of history was the time of Moses and towards the end of the desert wanderings of the children of Israel.

Balak was king of Moab. He was completely overawed and frightened by the story of Israel's recent victory over Sihon and Og, two Amorite kings, who tried to withstand Israel's progress. Balak imagined he could turn God's favour from Israel to his own nation if only he could find someone with sufficient weight or ability to change His mind. He looked for someone with supernatural powers to pronounce a powerful curse upon Israel to achieve their defeat (a scheme explained in detail in Numbers 22). He believed he had discovered the individual he wanted in Balaam, a money-grubbing heathen prophet.

Balaam was a diviner from the Euphrates. Having sought him out, Balak hired him to put a curse on the Israelites. At first Balaam appears to have been willing to go along with Balak's plan, but to his surprise found that he could not curse the Israelites. Instead of curses coming from Balaam's lips, Balak heard him pronounce blessings on Israel! The explanation was simple: God chose to intervene and make the soothsayer His instrument for this occasion, by putting His own message in Balaam's mouth. It must have been no small surprise to Balaam himself!

Balaam's first response to Balak, king of Moab, was that he could not curse Israel under any circumstances because God's determined purpose was to bless His people. 'How shall I curse whom God has not cursed? And how shall I denounce whom the LORD has not denounced?' (Numbers 23:8). Furious, Balak instructed Balaam to try again. Again the Lord met with him and put information for Balak into his mouth.

The second message was even more devastating for Balak and encouraging for Israel (Numbers 23:13-24). At its heart was Balaam's conclusion in verses 20 and 21: 'Behold, I have received a command to bless; He has blessed, and I cannot reverse it. He has not observed iniquity in Jacob, nor has He seen wickedness in Israel. The LORD his God is with him, and *the shout of a King* is among them.' Balaam declared the Israelites to be invincible because *the shout of a King* was among them.

What we have to take note of is the crucial fact that at this time in their history, the Israelites did not possess a visible king as most other nations did! Neither Saul nor David, the first human kings of God's people, had been born. Nevertheless, God's people did have a King! Better still, they possessed *the* King: invisible though He was to their physical eyes. The Lord Himself was their Sovereign. That was precisely what Balaam discerned when he said *'The shout of a King* is among them.'

Theme of the Psalms

Many Old Testament psalms proclaim God's Kingship. 'Oh, clap your hands, all you peoples! *Shout to God with the voice of triumph!* For the LORD Most High is awesome; *He is a great King over all the earth*' is how Psalm 47 begins (47: 1,2), meaningfully linking *the shout* with the theme of *God's Kingship.* The Psalm continues, 'God is the King of all the earth; sing praises with understanding. ... He is greatly exalted' (47: 7,9). Psalm 95 proclaims the LORD as *'the great king above all gods'* (95: 3), in whose hands and under whose authority is all creation (95: 4,5). The psalm significantly prefaces that statement at its beginning with the exhortation, 'Oh come, let us sing to the LORD! Let us *shout joyfully* to the Rock of our salvation' (95: 1). To have the LORD as King is to be part of His flock, the people who are under His care (95: 7). The divine Sovereign is the Saviour and Preserver of His people, worthy of their enthusiastic praise. Psalm 149 speaks of God's special Kingship over His redeemed people (149: 2).

The people of Israel could not have asked for a better King to rule over them, lead them, and take them into battle against their enemies. Best of all the Lord their King was with them. Israel was not simply blessed, and supported by God, but she enjoyed God's actual presence *among* her. That benefit distinguished her from any other group of people or nation. The Lord their King, although unseen, was present. He was not distant; rather He lived and reigned among them. With the inclusion again of the idea of the shout, Isaiah declares, '*Cry aloud and shout*, O inhabitant of Zion, for great is the Holy One of Israel *in your midst*' (Isaiah 12:6).

The symbol of the King's presence

God visibly indicated His presence with His people as their King by means of His tent or tabernacle. Through this portable sanctuary God expressed His dwelling among the Israelites during their forty years in the desert before they entered the promised land of Canaan.

When God's people encamped at Mount Sinai, they watched with trembling as a thick cloud covered the mountain, signifying God's coming down to speak to them. They then built the tabernacle at Moses' instruction. On the day of its completion, as they watched, 'the cloud covered the tabernacle of meeting, and the glory of the LORD filled the tabernacle. And Moses was not able to enter the tabernacle of meeting, because the cloud rested above it, and the glory of the LORD filled the tabernacle' (Exodus 40:34,35).

The tabernacle was the symbol of God's guiding and governing presence with His people. It went everywhere that Israel went. It 'was set up to be a suitable palace, with the ark as God's throne' (G.J. Wenham: *Numbers*, p.175). The ark, rectangular in shape, and covered with gold, served as a receptacle for the two tables of the Decalogue (the Ten Commandments), and for the pot of manna and Aaron's rod (Hebrews 9:4). It was the meeting place in the inner sanctuary where the Lord revealed His will to His servants (Exodus 25:22; 30:36).

It is an interesting and helpful thought that 'the camp in the wilderness was organised on the model of the Egyptian army with the companies encamped in square formation around the royal tent at the centre' (G.J. Wenham: *Numbers*, p.175). The secret of every deliverance and victory Israel knew was their King's presence with them, as Numbers 23:22a declares, '*God* brings them out of Egypt'.

Three pictures

Three pictures stand out in what Balaam said about *the shout of a King* among God's people. The illustrations are of a wild ox, powerless sorcerers and a lion. *A wild ox* indicates strength (Numbers 23:22; 24:8). Although the people of Israel may often have been small in number compared with their enemies, they possessed 'strength like a wild ox' (23: 22). Both *The New English Bible* and *Today's English Version* translate

Numbers 23:22 as referring to God's support for His people: 'He fights for them like a wild ox.' Balak, king of Moab, found himself powerless before them.

Powerless sorcerers express the truth of God's greater and unsurpassed power as the secret of Israel's protection against her enemies. Numbers 23:23 declares, 'There is no sorcery against Jacob, nor is there any divination against Israel.' The natural reaction of heathen monarchs and rulers wanting to overcome their enemies was to resort to sorcerers, to those who employed magic. They imagined that such individuals possessed supernatural power over others through the assistance of spirits and witchcraft. God's greater power meant that any plans Balak had to use evil forces against Israel were sure to fail.

A *lion* symbolises unresting persistence until victory is achieved (Numbers 23:24; 24:9). Of all the animals of the wild, the lion continues to be one of the most feared. With the Lord directing them, the people were said to rise like a lioness and to lift themselves like a lion, not resting until they had devoured their prey (Numbers 23:24). The conclusion was plain. *The King* was with them! What nation required a visible king when it had the invisible King of kings as its Sovereign?

Furthermore, not only was the Lord Jehovah Israel's King, but *His shout* was among them! The primary meaning of 'shout' is 'to raise a noise', either by calling out aloud or by means of a musical instrument like a horn or trumpet. The two meanings go together since, when the people shouted, they often accompanied the shout with the sounding of horns and trumpets.

The shout of homage

The first appropriate shout the people made was *the shout of homage*. 1 Samuel 4 provides an illustration, although not one to the credit of God's people. During the time of Eli's priesthood, the ark of the covenant resided at Shiloh, the sanctuary town where Eli lived. The town functioned as the capital city of Canaan in the period before Israel sought a human king. The tabernacle remained at Shiloh until the days of Samuel. 1 Samuel 4 describes how the Israelites went out to fight against the Philistines and were badly defeated, with about 4,000 of their men killed on the field of battle. They immediately asked, 'Why has the LORD defeated us today before the Philistines? Let us bring the ark of the covenant of the LORD from Shiloh to us, that when it comes among us it may save us from the hand of our enemies' (4: 3).

So the people sent to Shiloh to have the ark of the covenant of the Lord with them as they renewed their fight against their enemy. Sadly they did not seek God before taking such a decision, and spiritually they were out of touch with Him. The ark powerfully signified God's presence but it did not guarantee His presence if they were disobedient to Him. They resorted to a superstitious respect for the ark in place of a genuine trust in God. What is significant, however, is the manner in which they greeted the ark.

'When the ark of the covenant of the LORD came into the camp, all Israel shouted so loudly that the earth shook. Now when the Philistines heard the noise of the shout, they said, "What does the sound of this great shout in the camp of the Hebrews mean?" Then they understood that the ark of the LORD had come into the camp. So the Philistines were afraid, for they said, "God has come into the camp!"'(4: 5-7). Sadly, as we have indicated, the homage the Israelites then declared was only that of their lips and not that of the obedience of their lives. God requires both, and so He allowed their defeat. Nevertheless they were right to associate the shout of homage with *their King's presence*.

The act of homage at the coronation of Queen Elizabeth II in 1952 was a spine-tingling moment. The congregation in Westminster Abbey cried out as loudly as they could, 'God save the Queen!' When the Israelites' relationship to their Lord and King was right, they delighted to acknowledge Him. Without hesitation, and wholeheartedly, they declared, 'The LORD, He is God! The LORD, He is God!' They did this, for example, after Elijah's victory in God's Name over the prophets of Baal (1 Kings 18:39).

The shout of joy

The second appropriate shout was *the shout of joy* at God's presence among His people. 'Sing and rejoice, O daughter of Zion,' God declared through Zechariah, 'For behold, I am coming and I will dwell in your midst' (2:10). 'Sing' here, as often elsewhere, can equally well be translated 'shout'. Joy is the pre-eminent emphasis in the Old Testament regarding *the shout*, both in the psalms (i.e. Psalms 66:1; 81:1; 95:1; 98:4,6; 100:1) and the prophets (Isaiah 24:14; Jeremiah 31:7; Zechariah 9:9).

At the end of the second world war, crowds gathered outside Buckingham Palace in London. They shouted with joy every time the king and queen, with their family, appeared on the palace balcony. The great throng delighted in their presence. When a people or nation love their sovereign, they shout for joy every time they are conscious that he or she comes among them. The Israelites knew outstanding joy when they were aware that God their King was with them. They then declared to one another, 'The LORD has done great things for us, whereof we are glad' (Psalm 126:3). The greatness of the Holy One of Israel among them compelled them to rejoice and shout for joy.

The shout of faith and victory

The third appropriate shout was *the shout of faith* and *certain victory* because of the King's active leadership. Able leadership is the solution to most challenging situations in the corporate life of God's people, as well as generally in world affairs. When the Jews were sure that the Lord was leading them, they were able to shout praise to His Name in anticipation of the victory He would give them. Proclaiming His praise was their battle-cry or shout.

The account of Israel's overcoming of the city of Jericho illustrates this principle well. The Israelites had just entered the promised land. The first great difficulty that greeted them was Jericho, a walled city that must have seemed impregnable and impossible to capture.

Joshua, to all human appearances, was in charge. He must have been overawed by his responsibilities, having come only recently into his position of leadership after Moses' many years of command. Like any military commander, Joshua wanted to know the lie of the land. He took a private walk to survey the task before him. Suddenly 'he lifted his eyes and looked, and behold, a Man stood opposite him with His sword drawn in His hand. And Joshua went to Him and said to Him, "Are You for us or for our adversaries?" So He said, "No, but as Commander of the army of the LORD I have now come." And Joshua fell on his face to the earth and worshipped, and said to Him, "What does my Lord say to His servant?"

Then the Commander of the LORD's army said to Joshua, "Take your sandal off your foot, for the place where you stand is holy." And Joshua did so' (Joshua 5:13-15).

Many features of this encounter were highly significant. First, 'the Commander of the LORD's army' was plainly divine. Joshua was told that he stood on holy ground, even as Moses had been told at the burning bush (Exodus 3:5). This appearance to Joshua was none other than that of our Lord Jesus Christ, the Son of God, before His becoming flesh and making His dwelling among us—it was what we call a 'theophany'. We may view the theophanies as preparations for our Lord's Incarnation. They signified what He would be. They were different from His later appearing in a human body because they were visions of Him in human disguise whereas in the Incarnation He literally became flesh and shared our humanity, apart from sin. All the theophanies of the Old Testament showed something of His glory.

Second, Joshua was made to understand that it was not he—Joshua— who was in charge of Israel but the Lord, Israel's King. A sign of this was that the strategy for overcoming Jericho was not to be of Joshua's making but the Lord's. Detailed instructions were then given to Joshua by 'the Commander of the LORD's army' (Joshua 5:15; 6:2-5). The Israelites were to march around the city once a day with all the armed men, for six days. Though the priests would blow their trumpets, silence was to mark the rest of the people.

Joshua, following his orders, instructed the Israelites 'You shall not shout or make any noise with your voice, nor shall any word proceed out of your mouth, until the day I say to you, "Shout!" Then you shall shout' (Joshua 6:10). On the seventh day, at the moment Joshua told them to do so, the priests first blew a long blast on the trumpets. And then, at Joshua's instruction, 'the people *shouted*!' 'And it happened when the people heard the sound of the trumpet, and the people shouted with *a great shout*, that the wall fell down flat. Then the people went up into the city, every man straight before him, and they took the city' (Joshua 6:20). We can only guess at what they shouted, but we cannot be far wrong if we suggest that they shouted things like, 'The LORD has given us the city! The LORD is our King! The LORD is with us! Through the LORD we are sure of victory!' Jericho fell at *the shout of a King*!

The shout of a King was always among God's people as they followed His instructions. 'If God be for us,' they could have said, 'who can be against us?' *The shouts of homage, joy, faith and victory* were all included in the shout outside the walls of Jericho—the shout of their King. When *the shout of a King* was genuinely among His people, their morale could not have been better, and they were confident of accomplishing His will.

What of us?

The Church of Jesus Christ so easily loses sight of her King. The unbelieving world cannot understand our talking in such a way. How, it may ask, can you see One who is invisible to the human eye? Yet Christian believers know that it is possible to 'see' the King—to view Him with the eye of faith, with the eyes of the soul. That was Isaiah's experience when he went into the Temple in the sixth century BC (Isaiah 6:1; cf. John 12:41). It was also Stephen's as he was martyred by his fellow-Jews because of his testimony to Jesus (Acts 7:55-56). The Lord Jesus Christ promises to show Himself to obedient disciples (John 14:21).

One of the greatest tragedies in any local church fellowship is when it can go through all its seemingly Christian and religious activities, in the King's name, without the King Himself being present or even given room. This delights our ever-active spiritual enemy, Satan.

The Church may sadly forget that her richest benefit is her King's presence. The clue to the Church's growth and victories is not in her communicating skills or ability to learn techniques for numerical advancement from the world. Her secret of development and progress is in the assured presence of her Lord, as she rejoices in His Headship and submits to Him with joyful obedience. The church at Corinth had cause to learn this lesson. In spite of all the Corinthian Christians' pretensions about their possession of spiritual gifts and life, they needed to be reminded that what mattered most in their church life was that 'God is truly among you' (1 Corinthians 14:25).

A neglected aspect of our Lord's work

Losing sight of our King and His supreme place in the Church's life may be linked often with disregard for His Ascension, and its significance. I do not think it incorrect to describe the Ascension and in particular our Lord's continuing activity for us as neglected aspects of His work.

We rightly focus upon His Incarnation, the perfect life He lived, His authoritative teaching and amazing signs and miracles, culminating in His Death and Resurrection. Yet the final and crowning act of our Lord's earthly ministry was His Ascension. Both the *Gospels* and *The Acts of the Apostles* record it. It is worthy, therefore, of the most careful consideration. To overlook the Ascension is like reading an exciting book and failing to read the last chapter!

The Ascension may have been neglected because of the manner in which the Church's calendar is arranged. Easter Day is always celebrated on a Sunday, as is Whitsunday or Pentecost—and so they naturally receive the prominence they rightly deserve as Christians gather on a Sunday for worship and spiritual teaching. Ascension Day, however, forty days after Easter Day, falls on a Thursday, and for that reason it is often passed over since Christians do not regularly meet then. Nevertheless it is as important a day in the Church Calendar as any. I am cautious about emphasising the importance of one day over another, since this can so easily lead to superstitious respect. I would argue however that, if it is important to stir up our memories concerning the significance of some aspects of our Saviour's glorious redeeming work, so it is of others.

When the Church is spiritually healthy, her focus is upon her King. She then delights in, and longs for, His presence, and counts upon His activity on her behalf. This is entirely appropriate since God our Heavenly Father has given the Lord Jesus Christ, His Son and our Saviour, to be our Sovereign. To use New Testament language, God 'has delivered us from the power of darkness and translated us into the kingdom of the Son of His love' (Colossians 1:13). Our Saviour died that we might be able to enter and belong to His kingdom. He rose again to declare it open to all believers. Having shown Himself alive by many infallible proofs, He ascended to heaven to take His seat and place of authority there with the Father. The Church may declare with the psalmists, 'God has gone up with a shout, The LORD with the sound of a trumpet. ... Who is this King of glory? The LORD strong and mighty, the LORD mighty in battle' (Psalm 47:5; 24:8).

The sending of the Spirit

The Ascended Lord's presence with His Church is a benefit communicated by the Holy Spirit. Having ascended, Jesus sent His Spirit that His people might be always assured that He is *with* them and *for* them. The Spirit uniquely makes the Lord Jesus' presence real to us. *The King is among you* the Spirit assures us. The King has promised, 'Where two or three are gathered together in My name, I am there in the midst of them' (Matthew 18:20). His presence and His *shout* are our spiritual birthright. As we enter into the richness of our spiritual inheritance as His people, so both His presence and shout are ours. As His Church, we need to know *the shout of a King* among us. That shout means that our spiritual focus is upward, our faith bright, our obedience active and our progress glorifying to our King.

Our task

We cannot study and meditate upon the Ascension without also considering what the Lord Jesus Christ does *now* for His people. The New Testament exhortation to fix our eyes on Jesus underlines the relevance of what He does at this present time on our account. To understand more of this provides unique spiritual encouragement and joy, both of which are indispensable for living the Christian life as God intends, and for the Church to know *the shout of her King*. The right place to begin is with the promises and anticipations of the Ascension.

Promises and anticipations of the Ascension

The Ascension of our Lord Jesus Christ was promised and anticipated in the Old Testament, and then confirmed beforehand by our Lord Jesus Christ.

Testaments of promise

We may be so accustomed to the Bible's two parts—the Old and the New Testaments—that we lose sight of the significance of the word 'covenant', an alternative word for 'testament'. The Old Testament unfolds the range of promises God made with the Jewish people, although always with non-Jews in mind (e.g. Genesis 17:5,6). The New Testament amplifies the promises God makes to men and women of all races—whether Jews or non-Jews—in and through His Son Jesus Christ.

Most promises tend to be important and that is especially true of those that God makes. God's first promise of salvation is in Genesis 3:15. He said to the serpent, an instrument of the devil, who deceived Eve, 'I will put enmity between you and the woman, and between your seed and her Seed; He shall bruise your head, and you shall bruise His heel.' This was the acorn of God's saving promises: all that followed were in embryo here.

Abraham received God's promises as the father of the Jewish race, and the spiritual father of all who believe God's promises and are justified through the Lord Jesus Christ. God's spiritual offspring—His true children—are those who believe His promises in His Son (Romans 9:8). A paramount pledge of God to Abraham was, 'I will establish My covenant between Me and you and your descendants after you in their generations, for an everlasting covenant, to be God to you and your descendants after you' (Genesis 17:7).

When we make promises, we may do so lightly, or, if not lightly, without appreciating how difficult their achievement may be. Since God makes promises with infinite wisdom, their accomplishment is always certain. No doubt exists about His ability to carry out what He promises since He sees the end from the beginning and possesses almighty power.

Infallible predictions

God's promises are infallible predictions. Sometimes He may put a long date on their performance, but that in no way alters their certainty. His divine character stands behind them. Abraham discovered that the Lord 'gives life to the dead and calls those things which do not exist as though they did' (Romans 4:17). The sureness of God's promises outweighs all natural improbabilities (Romans 4:19); they do not fail (Romans 9:6).

God's promises in the Old Testament led to the expectation of the coming of the Messiah, our Lord Jesus Christ, as the Hope of the ages. They indicated His divine nature. They anticipated the Saviour of Israel bringing both judgment and salvation. Essentially He was the One who *comes*. Great stress was placed upon His coming (Genesis 49:10), and His coming on behalf of His people (Zechariah 9:9), for He came up as a shoot from the stump of Jesse (Isaiah 11:1). Indication was given of His exceptional birth (Isaiah 7:14; 9:6) and its unique purposes. 'A Star shall come out of Jacob; a Sceptre shall rise out of Israel' (Numbers 24:17). He came in God's Name and purpose (Micah 5:2), to fulfil His sovereign designs and commissions (Zechariah 3:8,9). He is raised up (Jeremiah 23:5) and placed over His people as their Shepherd (Ezekiel 34:23). Furthermore, He is to come yet again in majesty (Daniel 7:13,14) to judge to the ends of the earth and to bring salvation to those who acknowledge Him (Psalm 2:8-12).

The Old Testament is full of hope, especially as it focuses upon the *coming* King. It provides therefore the right place for us to start. It always looks forward, implying that it relates to a period of history in which much is temporary, while it waits for what will be permanent.

The prophets

God's promises, if not given directly to individuals like Abraham and Moses, were usually delivered by God's spokesmen, His prophets. We are accustomed to 'spokes-people' in our contemporary world. We read, or hear it reported, 'A government spokesperson stated such and such.' What the spokesman and spokeswoman say is what those whom they represent wish us to hear. The prophets declared what God wants us to know and understand.

Besides being God's spokes-man, the prophets saw things in the future from a distance. They were look-out men on behalf of God's people. They were like sentries, or watchmen. Children are sometimes on tiptoes with excitement before an important event. Those with prophetic gift in the Old Testament period were frequently on 'tiptoes' with anticipation as they foresaw the coming of the Lord's Anointed, the Messiah. Peter expresses their sense of joyful anticipation in his first letter, 'Of this salvation the prophets have inquired and searched diligently, who prophesied of the grace that would come to you, searching what, or what manner of time, the Spirit of Christ who was in them was indicating when He testified beforehand the sufferings of Christ and the glories that would follow. To them it was revealed that, not to themselves, but to us they were ministering the things which now have been reported to you through those who have preached the gospel to you by the Holy Spirit sent from heaven—things which angels desire to look into' (1 Peter 1:10-12).

Significantly, the prophets saw, and predicted, two particular features of the Messiah's destiny: *His sufferings and His glory*. They could not always determine which was to come first. The two were frequently expressed together, but with glory coming more often after suffering. If I hold up two sheets of paper upon one of which I write 'sufferings' and on the other 'glory', it may be difficult, if not impossible, from a distance, to be sure which piece of paper is closer to someone who stands fifty yards or even less from me. When we view a landscape from a distance, we cannot always be sure which feature in the topography comes first until we walk or drive up to it. So it was with what the prophets saw from a distance. Nevertheless, both suffering and glory they did see clearly! That glory is now our focus.

A prophetic chain
The Ascension was a vital link in a chain of fulfilled Old Testament promises and prophecies concerning the Messiah. Each link is essential to the complete chain. The Ascension was an indispensable part of God's promises concerning His Son. We describe a number of psalms as Messianic in that they looked forward to the Saviour's coming, and some of these especially anticipated His Ascension. Usually they had an immediate reference to the period of history in which they were written, although not

necessarily so. We cannot always identify contemporary circumstances to which they might have applied.

Even as our Lord's birth, ministry, death and Resurrection were prophesied, so also were His Ascension and what follows it. It is in the Messianic psalms that particular focus is upon the Ascension and its significance. Such psalms point without any possibility of doubt to the Messiah's deity, for His eternal Godhead is basic to them. They all relate to the Messiah as King. As we consider them in detail, we soon recognise that they could never apply merely to a human king. Psalm 72 is an excellent example. It inspired two well used hymns in the English language—Isaac Watts' *Jesus shall reign* and James Montgomery's *Hail to the Lord's Anointed*. While the psalm initially referred to the reigning king, its fulfilment is possible only for the Messiah. 'He will judge Your people with righteousness, and Your poor with justice. ... He will bring justice to the poor of the people; He will save the children of the needy, and will break in pieces the oppressor. ... He shall have dominion also from sea to sea, and from the River to the ends of the earth. ... Yes, all kings shall bow down before Him; all nations shall serve Him. ... And men shall be blessed in Him; all nations shall call Him blessed' (Psalm 72: 2, 4, 8, 11, 17).

The Messiah rises above any historical reality of human kingship. This King, to whom the peoples will render obedience, receives sovereignty over everything. He blesses all the families of the earth. Psalm 2:12 unmistakably identifies Him as God's Son, who determines men and women's everlasting salvation or destruction. Psalm 45:6-7 names Him as God and Psalm 72:5,7,17 ascribes eternity of dominion to Him. Psalm 110:1 depicts Him as the Lord of His people who sits at the right hand of God.

The latter psalm, Psalm 110, is a vital psalm about the Ascension. It begins, 'The LORD said to my Lord, "Sit at My right hand, till I make Your enemies Your footstool."' Luther chose it as the subject of his spring sermons in 1538. He declared, 'This is the high and chief Psalm of our dear Lord Jesus Christ, in which His Person, and His Resurrection, Ascension, and His whole Kingdom are so clearly and powerfully set forth, that nothing of a similar kind is to be found in all the writings of the Old Testament. It is therefore meet and right that it should be sung and expounded at such festivals of our Lord as Easter, Ascension, and Whitsuntide.' Luther may have exaggerated a little! Nevertheless, the New

Testament's use of the psalm supports his conviction concerning its importance.

Psalm 110's author was David. We may affirm his authorship not only because of the heading given in the book of psalms itself—'A Psalm of David'—but because of the confirmation the New Testament provides (Matthew 22:41ff; Mark 12:36,37; Luke 20:42,43,44). Matthew records the discussion Jesus had with the Pharisees concerning the question, 'Whose Son is the Christ?' 'While the Pharisees were gathered together, Jesus asked them, saying, "What do you think about the Christ? Whose Son is He?" They said to Him, "The Son of David." He said to them, "How then does David in the Spirit call Him 'Lord,' saying: 'The LORD said to my Lord, "Sit at My right hand, till I make Your enemies Your footstool"'? If David then calls him 'Lord', how is He his son?" And no one was able to answer Him a word, nor from that day on did anyone dare question Him any more' (Matthew 22:41-46). The New Testament confirms it elsewhere as a Messianic psalm (for example, Acts 2:34,35). We are right to apply it therefore to the Person of our Lord Jesus Christ (1 Corinthians 15:25; Hebrews 1:13; 10:12,13).

Three pictures

Three pictures of the Messiah stand out in Psalm 110: He is *King* (1,2), *Priest* (4) and *Judge* (6). The theme is the appointment of the Messiah to all three offices. We begin with *His Kingship* and the formal splendours and special equipment that are His. No honour or emblem of authority can be too great for this King. Four symbols of His majesty are indicated: *a throne* (1), *a footstool* (2), *a sceptre* (3) *and an army* (4).

First, a *throne* is a royal seat of authority or power. The summons to the Messiah to 'sit at My right hand' is an invitation to join the Father on His throne. A throne expresses the exalted status of the one who sits upon it, and is an emblem here of our Saviour's unsurpassed majesty. He 'is the supreme Agent of the unimaginable Power on whom the universe depends' (C. S. Lewis).

Second, a *footstool* is the natural accompaniment of a throne, for upon it the Sovereign rests his feet. Solomon's throne, for example, 'had six steps, with a footstool of gold, which were fastened to the throne' (2

Chronicles 9:18). In the ancient world victorious monarchs, as a display of their triumph, placed their feet on the necks of conquered enemies (Joshua 10:24). The Messiah's footstool is a pledge of His ultimate triumph over all who fight against Him and His kingdom.

Third, the *sceptre*, a short decorated stick carried by rulers at important ceremonies, is a further symbol of office (110: 2). Psalm 2 speaks of the Messiah ruling His enemies 'with an iron sceptre', and His dashing 'them in pieces like a potter's vessel' (2:9). His sceptre represents His ability to control all who choose to oppose His rule.

Fourth, His *army* is an army of volunteers, the Father's gift, whom we may identify as the elect. They are described as 'volunteers' or as 'willing'. Besides being willing to be saved by His righteousness, they are willing to take on His yoke (cf. Matthew 11:29, 30) and to bear His Cross. A youthful army, marked like the dew by freshness and vitality, streams to His royal banner from all nations.

The Messiah's majesty is prominent. The LORD Jehovah says to Him as the divinely appointed King, 'Sit at My right hand, till I make Your enemies Your footstool' (110:1). The Messiah, our Lord Jesus, rules by His Father's decree over both His own people and His enemies. He is told, 'The LORD shall send the rod of Your strength out of Zion. Rule in the midst of Your enemies! ... The Lord is at Your right hand; He shall execute kings in the day of His wrath' (110:2,5).

The King is also *the Priest*. The ancient world was accustomed to priests in a way we are not. A priest always stood between God and the men and women he represented. Above all else, he had to be acceptable to God, and ideally, therefore, appointed by Him. The Messiah possesses both qualifications, uniquely and eternally. The Lord says to Him as Priest, 'You are a priest for ever according to the order of Melchizedek' (4). Melchizedek was the mysterious king and priest of 'God Most High' who appeared on the scene in Genesis 14 when Abraham (then called Abram) returned from rescuing Lot. Melchizedek then disappeared, with nothing said about his birth or death, ancestry or descent. These features indicated his superiority to Abraham, and, by implication, to the Aaronic priesthood descended from him.

The Messiah's role as Priest was later the major theme of the writer of the Letter to the Hebrews. He shows how the promise of a priesthood, superior to that of Aaron, solemnly brought into being, and constituted not to be changed, pointed to the putting aside of the Levitical priesthood. The promise receives fulfilment only in the Person and work of our Lord Jesus.

The Messiah who is King and Priest is also the *Judge* (110:6). His dominion as Messiah is world-wide, and so are His power and authority to administer justice and determine men and women's eternal destiny. The psalm sets forth our Lord's judicial reign, or His rule as Judge, a theme taken up in the Book of Revelation (19:11-21). His wrath is that of the just Judge. He will crush kings and rulers (110:5)—that is to say, those who have governed throughout the ages, and have been responsible for horrible crimes and dreadful atrocities upon humankind. Justice will be done, and seen to be done.

We see this psalm's importance in that it is quoted directly and indirectly in the New Testament more than any other (cf. Mark 16:19; Acts 5:31; 7:55f; Romans 8:34; 1 Corinthians 15:24ff; Ephesians 1:20; Colossians 3:1; Hebrews 1:3; 8:1; 10:12f; 1 Peter 3:22). On the Day of Pentecost, filled with the Spirit, Peter proclaimed Jesus' Resurrection, and testified by means of this psalm to His Ascension and Exaltation. 'This Jesus God has raised up, of which we are all witnesses. Therefore being exalted to the right hand of God, and having received from the Father the promise of the Holy Spirit, He poured out this which you now see and hear. For David did not ascend into the heavens, but he says himself: "The LORD said to my Lord, 'Sit at My right hand, till I make Your enemies Your footstool.'" Therefore let all the house of Israel know assuredly that God has made this Jesus, whom you crucified, both Lord and Christ' (Acts 2:32-36). With absolute confidence, through the understanding the Holy Spirit gave him, Peter applied Psalm 110 to our Lord Jesus as the Messiah. He identified the psalm's reference to the Messiah's sitting at God's right hand with Jesus' exaltation at the Ascension.

Psalm 24

Other psalms speak of the Ascension, and particularly Psalm 24. It had its first reference to the people and events of the time when it was written, and a forward allusion to the Messiah. This is a wonder of the Holy Spirit's inspiration of Scripture. Psalms clearly sometimes have a double meaning. The writer of Psalm 24 wrote about a contemporary event, but under the influence of the Holy Spirit, he conveyed an even more important truth about Jesus Christ.

The psalm seems to have been composed originally for a ceremonial occasion, such as the Feast of Ingathering and Tabernacles when the Jewish people annually declared God's Kingship. It was kept for seven days from the fifteenth to the twenty-second day of the seventh month (September-October). It came at the end of the year when they gathered in the fruits of working in the fields, and was one of the three annual festivals that every male was required to attend. The name 'Feast of Tabernacles (or booths)' arose from the requirement for everyone born an Israelite to live in temporary shelters made of boughs of trees and branches of palm trees for the seven days of the feast (Leviticus 23:42).

The ark, symbolising the LORD Jehovah's presence (Psalm 132:8), ascended Mount Zion in procession, there to be challenged, admitted and finally acclaimed with the cry, 'The LORD reigns' (Psalm 93:1). Out of this festival arose an anticipation for the future when the Lord would gloriously rule over His people—an expectation the Lord Jesus Christ would make a glorious reality.

Traditionally the Church has sung Psalm 24 on Ascension Day, especially because of verses 7-10: 'Lift up your heads, O you gates! And be lifted up, you everlasting doors! And the King of glory shall come in. Who is this King of glory? The LORD strong and mighty, the LORD mighty in battle. Lift up your heads, O you gates! And lift them up, you everlasting doors! And the King of glory shall come in. Who is this King of glory? The LORD of hosts, He is the King of glory.' God's dwelling-place is pictured as an ancient walled city with gates through which alone we may gain entrance. None may enter these gates without God's approval, for His city is holy. Christians throughout the centuries have delighted to recognise in this psalm a representation of heaven's triumph and welcome at the return of our Lord Jesus there at His Ascension. He went out of that city to become the Saviour we need. He became man, as He was born of a virgin, through the Holy Spirit's work of conception in Mary's womb. He has now returned to that city as both God and man, bearing the scars and fruits of His Cross.

The background of conflict in the psalm may be explained by the war between heaven and earth ever since the fall of the angels, Adam and Eve's rebellion, and all that has followed. It was in view of this that God sent forth Jesus, the Achiever of our salvation, prefigured centuries before by people such as Joshua and David, to conquer Satan and all his works, and to remove his power. By His atoning death God the Son accomplished this great work. Then, having been raised from the dead, He entered the glory that He had left for a while. All heaven rejoiced at His triumphant return.

Early Christian writers pondered why the question should be repeated, 'Who is this King of glory?' (24:10). Their conclusion was that it was because of the sight of Jesus as One who had been crucified, making it difficult for the inhabitants of heaven to recognise Him. This is fanciful speculation, with no substance in the text. Nevertheless it is not an unhelpful thought to prompt our worship and amazement. Describing God's amazing disclosure of His plan of salvation in the Old Testament, Peter expresses heaven's surprise when he comments, 'things which angels desire to look into' (1 Peter 1:12).

Gregory of Nazianus and Gregory of Nyssa, lived in the province of Cappadocia in the second half of the fourth century. Together with Basil of Caesarea they had a profound influence in the Church, especially in its understanding of the Trinity. Gregory of Nazianus urged, 'Join yourselves to the angels who escort Him or those who receive Him. Bid the gates raise their lintels to receive Him whose stature is now exalted by virtue of His passion. To those who are now in doubt because He bears in His Ascension a body and tokens of His passion, which He had not when He came down, and who therefore enquire, Who is this King of glory? reply that it is the Lord strong and mighty' (Or.XLV.25). Gregory of Nyssa suggested that 'When Christ ascends our guardians form a procession for Him, and command the hyper cosmic powers to open the heavens that He may be adored there once more. But they did not recognise Him because He has put on the poor coat of human nature, and His garments are red from the winepress of our sins. And this time it is they who cry: "Who is this King of glory?"' (Or.Asc).

Other psalms

Psalm 47 has a reference to our Lord's Ascension. Verse 5 is an allusion to 2 Samuel 6:15 where the Jews brought up the ark to the city of David to make that city God's abode: 'God has gone up with a shout, the LORD with the sound of a trumpet.' God is pictured here ascending His earthly throne.

Psalm 68 is yet another psalm written with an immediate situation in view, but with relevance to the Ascension. It is thought to have been written for David's procession with the ark from 'the house of Obed-Edom to the City of David with gladness' (2 Samuel 6:12). The ark was viewed as the throne of the invisible God (Psalm 132:8). The procession with the ark was a preview in miniature of a far greater ascension. Verses 17 and 18 of Psalm 68 read: 'The chariots of God are twenty thousand, even thousands of thousands; the Lord is among them as in Sinai, in the Holy Place. You have ascended on high, You have led captivity captive; You have received gifts among men, even among the rebellious, that the LORD God might dwell there.' However we view these words, they speak of the infinite nature of God's resources, His incomparable riches.

The Old Testament's anticipation in the Messianic psalms of our Lord's Ascension and Exaltation underline the importance of these two events. Whatever the original circumstances and significance to those who first heard or read the psalms, the early Church, enlightened by the Spirit Jesus promised, saw in them the triumph and glory of their Ascended Lord. They had good grounds for this use of the Old Testament, for on the Emmaus Road the Lord Jesus Himself said to the two disciples He met there, '"Ought not the Christ to have suffered these things and to enter into His glory?" And beginning at Moses and all the Prophets, He expounded to them in all the Scriptures the things concerning Himself' (Luke 24:26,27).

Other prophetic anticipations

Using the insight the New Testament provides, we find many other Old Testament anticipations of the Messiah's Exaltation. It is no surprise to find such expectation in the Servant passages of Isaiah. 'He shall see the travail of His soul, and be satisfied. By His knowledge My righteous Servant shall justify many' (Isaiah 53:11). 'He shall see His seed' (Isaiah 53:10). God 'will divide Him a portion with the great' (Isaiah 53:12). 'His name will be called

Wonderful, Counsellor, Mighty God, Everlasting Father, Prince of Peace. Of the increase of His government and peace there will be no end, upon the throne of David and over His kingdom, to order it and establish it with judgment and justice from that time forward, even forever' (Isaiah 9:6,7). 'A Root of Jesse ... shall stand as a banner to the people; for the Gentiles shall seek Him, and His resting place shall be glorious' (Isaiah 11:10). The words of Isaiah 52:13 are particularly appropriate: 'Behold, My servant shall deal prudently, He shall be exalted and extolled and be very high.' *Exalted, extolled*, and *be very high (raised, lifted up* and *highly exalted*, NIV), express in the correct order the Resurrection, Ascension and Exaltation of the Lord Jesus. They point to the unimaginable dignity of our King.

Jesus' anticipation and teaching about His Ascension and Exaltation

Our Lord Himself foretold His Ascension. John's gospel contains at least nine references to it, most of them in the upper room conversations He had with His disciples immediately before His betrayal and crucifixion (John 6:62; 7:33; 14:12,28; 16:5,10,17,28; 20:17). The first recorded instance was after the feeding of the five thousand, as described by John. Jesus rebuked the crowd that followed Him after the miracle because of their preoccupation with physical and material considerations rather than spiritual. He chose to emphasise that His kingdom is not of this world, and He asked, 'What then if you should see the Son of Man ascend where He was before?' (John 6:62). Here His Ascension stood for all the events begun by His Crucifixion. If they stumbled at what He said to them then, how they would stumble at His Cross and all that followed! From the beginning, therefore, He taught that the Ascension was an event men and women were to see, and that it would mark His return to heaven and to His Father.

In John's next chapter, speaking this time to His critics, Jesus said, 'I shall be with you a little while longer, and then I go to Him who sent Me. You will seek Me and not find Me, and where I am you cannot come' (John 7:33,34). The implication here is that His Ascension signalled the accomplishment of His mission—the task He was sent into the world by His Father to accomplish.

At Jesus' Transfiguration Moses and Elijah talked to Him of His 'decease', literally His 'exodus' (Luke 9:31). At first the use of the word 'exodus' seems strange, but it was highly significant. The Exodus delivered Israel from slavery. By His 'exodus' the Lord Jesus delivered His people from far worse slavery—their bondage to sin which leads to death. The Exodus was a moment of glorious triumph for the Jews, and so too was Jesus' death viewed in the light of the Resurrection and Ascension.

In His intimate talks with the disciples, the Lord Jesus stressed the necessity of His return to the Father. He said, 'But now I go away to Him who sent Me, and none of you asks Me, "Where are You going?" But because I have said these things to you, sorrow has filled your heart. Nevertheless I tell you the truth. It is to your advantage that I go away; for if I do not go away, the Helper will not come to you; but if I depart, I will send Him to you. And when He has come, He will convict the world of sin, and of righteousness, and of judgment' (John 16:5-8). Our Lord amplified here the necessity for the Ascension. It was for the disciples' good—and ours—because as a consequence the Holy Spirit was to come as the Helper and Convicter. He was to strengthen them and give power and authority to their preaching.

Jesus promised the Spirit would convict men and women of right-eousness because He went to the Father (16:10). So far as the world was concerned the Cross was either Jesus' just deserts (if an impostor) or a dreadful mistake and waste (if God's Son). His Resurrection and return to the Father's throne proved that all that Jesus had said and done was right—that is to say, righteous. Had that not been so, the Father would not have taken Him into glory. The Holy Spirit shows and convinces us of this. He then goes on to teach us that we ourselves can only be right with God, and accepted by Him, if Jesus' righteousness is imputed to us as we trust in Him and His saving work for sinners.

On Jesus' arrest and trial before the chief priests and the whole Sanhedrin (the Jewish Supreme Court), the High Priest said to Him, 'I adjure You by the living God that You tell us if You are the Christ, the Son of God.' Jesus said to him, 'It is as you said. Nevertheless, I say to you, hereafter you will see the Son of Man sitting at the right hand of the Power, and coming on the clouds of heaven' (Matthew 26:63,64). In mentioning His 'sitting at the right hand of the Power', our Lord clearly referred to Psalm 110:1, and indicated that His Ascension and Exaltation are the prelude to His return in glory.

The final reference our Lord made to the Ascension was at His Resurrection when Mary of Magdala sought to clutch hold of Him at her joy at seeing Him alive from the dead. 'Jesus said to her, "Do not cling to Me, for I have not yet ascended to My Father; but go to My brethren, and say to them, 'I am ascending to My Father and your Father, and to My God and your God'"' (John 20:17). Mary's natural reaction was to hold on to Him, as never to let Him go. Stressing again His return to His Father, our Lord indicated that old relationships, based upon physical sight and presence, were now to be replaced by a more intimate and spiritual relationship with Him, and one available continuously for all disciples everywhere. As Paul put it in a different way, 'From now on, we regard no one according to the flesh. Even though we have known Christ according to the flesh, yet now we know Him thus no longer' (2 Corinthians 5:16). Our present relationship to the Lord Jesus is spiritual, not physical. Since the Ascension, our Saviour is physically remote, but spiritually near. We shall consider the implications of this in greater detail later. Our purpose in this chapter has been to establish the Old Testament's eager anticipation of our Saviour's Ascension and Exaltation, and His own teaching concerning them to His disciples.

The Ascension and its proclamation of Jesus' identity

Each writer of the four gospels determined the appropriate ending for his gospel record. Matthew and Mark significantly conclude with our Lord Jesus' great commission (Matthew 28:18-20; Mark 16:15,16), with the disciples then going obediently into all the world with the message of salvation. John's approach is different. He draws his account to a close with Jesus commissioning the disciples in the upper room (John 20:19-23), and he finishes with Peter's reinstatement and recommissioning (John 21:15-23).

Luke ends his gospel purposefully with the Ascension (24:50-53), and we may discern the probable reasons. His plan was 'to set in order a narrative' for Theophilus, the first intended reader he had in mind as he wrote (Luke 1:3). His intention was to record the facts of Jesus' life, as handed down by 'eyewitnesses and ministers of the word' (1:2). He had carefully investigated 'all things from the very first' (1:3). The disciples—his main informants—were eyewitnesses of Jesus' Ascension.

Furthermore, Luke wanted Theophilus—and other readers, including ourselves—to know 'the certainty of those things' in which we 'were instructed' (1:4), and the Ascension is one such certainty. That Luke should give such an important place to the Ascension is even more impressive because theologians and secular historians recognise him to be meticulous with regard to historical detail and accuracy. There is however another reason for Luke ending his gospel with the Ascension. He is also the author of what we know as *The Acts of the Apostles*, and it is with the Ascension that Luke begins that book. The Ascension links his two writings together.

Forty days after the Resurrection

The Ascension took place forty days following the Resurrection. Writing of Jesus and the apostles at the beginning of *Acts*, Luke tells us that 'He ... presented Himself alive after His suffering by many infallible proofs, being seen by them during forty days and speaking of the things pertaining to the kingdom of God' (Acts 1:3).

'Forty' is a significant number in the Bible. For forty days the flood came upon the earth in the time of Noah (Genesis 7:17; 8:6). Moses stayed twice on Mount Sinai forty days and forty nights when he received God's instructions for His people, and in particular the Ten Commandments (Exodus 24:18; 34:28; Deuteronomy 9:9,11,18,25; 10:10). The spies that Moses sent out to explore the promised land of Canaan took forty days to accomplish it (Numbers 13:25). At the beginning of His ministry, the Lord Jesus spent forty days in the desert being tempted by the devil (Matthew 4:2; Mark 1:13; Luke 4:2). Forty is the most frequently used round number in the Bible and conveys the idea of completeness.

There are questions about Jesus' resurrection appearances during those forty days before the Ascension that we cannot answer, and in particular, 'Where was He during those days?' Many have speculated, but the absence of comment in the New Testament makes it a matter of conjecture, for which there is little if any point. What is plain is that each appearance was at Jesus' initiative. In John 21:1 and 14 the Lord Jesus 'showed Himself' and in Acts 1:3, the Lord Jesus 'presented Himself alive' to His disciples. Only in Acts 10:40 is God the Father's initiative indicated, when Peter said to Cornelius and his household, 'Him God raised up on the third day, and showed Him openly.' This mention of God the Father is a reminder that the Bible regularly ascribes the initiative in the plan of salvation to the First Person of the Trinity. However the initiative in the individual appearances of the risen Jesus was His own.

The preposition translated in Acts 1:3 as 'during' means intermittently rather than continuously throughout. During the forty days Jesus explained truths about His kingdom the apostles had not previously understood, and He clarified especially the spiritual nature of His kingdom.

These periods of conversation with their Risen Lord were invaluable to the apostles. They convinced them of the physical reality of His Resurrection. They were able to perceive the meaning of what He had been teaching them in the previous three years but which they had been slow to grasp. They were able to ask questions and understand the essential message and commission by which their Lord's work was—and is—to be advanced.

Paul's unique statements in 1 Corinthians 15:5-7 and the record of the four gospels enable us to identify nine or ten appearances of Jesus to His disciples, some in Judea and others in Galilee. The Ascension marked the end of Jesus' intermittent visits to His followers. It was a transition point. His Ascension means He is no longer physically upon earth. It was like the lowering of the curtain at the end of a play: if you were not certain before, you are now sure that it is complete!

The Mount of Olives

The Mount of Olives was the scene of the Ascension (Luke 24:50; Acts 1:12). The Garden of Gethsemane was probably at its foot on the western slope. The Mount of Olives is part of the highest range of hills east of Jerusalem, with a small ridge of four summits overlooking the city. It is sometimes called Olivet. In the first century it was thickly wooded with olive trees. Luke indicates that Jesus led the disciples out to near Bethany, a village on the Mount of Olives. This was the last stopping place for pilgrims on the road from Jericho to Jerusalem. If we put together Luke's two statements that the Lord Jesus led them out 'as far as Bethany' (Luke 24:50), and that where they were was 'near Jerusalem, a Sabbath day's journey' (about three-quarters of a mile, the maximum people were supposed to walk on the Sabbath), it occurred approximately halfway between Jerusalem and Bethany (Luke 24:50; Acts 1:12).

This location was an area Jesus visited often during His ministry, not least for prayer and rest (Matthew 21:1; 24:3; 26:30; Mark 11:1; 13:3; 14:26; Luke 19:29,37; 21:37; John 8:1). We read in Luke 22:39, 'He went to the Mount of Olives, as He was accustomed, and His disciples also followed Him.' From this vantage point He could view all Jerusalem, the city He loved, but in which He was so cruelly treated. In his commentary on the first three gospels, Calvin wrote, 'His ascension was ... from the Mount of Olives, ... whence He had descended to undergo the ignominy of the Cross, that He might ascend the heavenly throne ... the King of glory and the Judge of the world' (*Synoptic Gospels*, III, p.392f).

The significant blessing

The apostles witnessed the Ascension after the Lord Jesus finished talking to them (Mark 16:19). He then significantly lifted up His hands to bless them (Luke 24:50,51). A last memory or recollection we have of seeing someone whom we respect and love always lives with us. It was *while* He was blessing them that He left them (Luke 24:51).

The lifting up of the hands was a recognised priestly gesture. Luke records in the first chapter of his gospel how the people waited in vain for a priest named Zechariah to appear at the porch of the Temple (Luke 1:21). The reason for their having to wait longer than was expected was the appearance of the angel Gabriel to Zechariah. Zechariah was made dumb because of his unbelief, until God's promise of a son, John the Baptist, was fulfilled. What the people waited for was Zechariah's raising of his hands high over his head to bless them in God's Name (*Mishnah*, *Tamid* 7:2).

The Book of Numbers records the words of blessing the priests were to pronounce upon God's people. It was a function of the priesthood to bless in God's Name the worshipping community (Leviticus 9:22,23; Deuteronomy 10:8). The benediction came not from the priests but from the Lord as Numbers 6:24-26 eloquently expresses: 'The LORD bless you and keep you; the LORD make His face shine upon you and be gracious to you; the LORD lift up His countenance upon you, and give you peace.'

Jesus' lifting up of His hands to bless His disciples was a remarkably appropriate action. Raising His hands after the pattern of the Levitical priests to bless His waiting people, He did what the priests could never do: the priests could pray a blessing, the Lord Jesus can bestow blessing. All God's blessings come to us through our Lord Jesus Christ. Paul rightly declares, 'Blessed be the God and Father of our Lord Jesus Christ, who has blessed us with every spiritual blessing in the heavenly places in Christ' (Ephesians 1:3).

It was in the act of blessing the disciples that the Lord Jesus left them. They were not conscious of His blessing ending because it never does! His blessing of His people is still unfinished! As Thomas Watson put it in the seventeenth century, 'He did not leave them houses and lands, but He left them His blessing' (T. Watson, *A Body of Divinity*, p.143). The Lord Jesus is the Lord of the uplifted hands and the unfinished blessing. The intended pattern of Christian experience is that from the generous bounty of our Lord Jesus Christ's grace we should receive 'grace upon grace' or, as the NIV translates it, 'one blessing after another' (John 1:16). We see here how we are to think properly of our Ascended Lord: He lives to bless His Church. As Samuel Medley's hymn, *I know that my Redeemer lives* puts it, 'He lives to bless me with His love.'

Taken up into heaven

With this act of blessing the Lord Jesus was taken up in full view of the disciples into heaven, and a cloud took Him out of their sight (Luke 24:50, 51; Acts 1:9). The visibility of the Ascension is stressed: while the disciples 'watched, He was taken up … And while they looked steadfastly towards heaven … He went up' (Acts 1:9,10).

Objections to the Ascension have been made on the grounds that the accounts rest upon outdated views of heaven as a place above our heads. C. S. Lewis made the interesting suggestion that it is not an accident that the ideas of God and Heaven and the blue sky should be blended. 'The huge dome of the sky is of all things sensuously perceived the most like infinity. And when God made space and worlds that move into space, and clothed our world with air, and gave us such eyes and such imaginations as we have, He knew what the sky would mean to us. And since nothing in His work is accidental, if He knew, He intended. We cannot be certain that this was not indeed one of the chief purposes for which Nature was created; still less that it was not one of the chief reasons why the withdrawal was allowed to affect human senses as a movement upwards' (*Miracles*, p. 162).

Three words for 'heaven' exist in Hebrew so that we may refer precisely to the sky, the universe or God's dwelling place. Greek, the language of the New Testament, combines all three senses in one word. At the Ascension the Lord Jesus went up into the sky, traversed through space, into the presence of God. While we cannot define heaven geographically, objections to our view of it, as above us, are beside the point because the symbolism is natural to us. Our Lord Jesus is said to have 'lifted up His eyes to heaven' when He prayed (John 17:1). He teaches us to pray, 'Our Father in heaven' and 'Your will be done on earth as it is in heaven' (Matthew 6:9,10). When individuals like Stephen and Paul later had visions of the ascended Jesus, they significantly looked upwards (Acts 7:55; 9:3; 22:6; 26:13). If nothing else, when we refer to the Ascension, we are expressing the truth that the base of our Saviour's present operations is no longer here but with the Father in glory. He moved away from earth, even as He will come to earth at His return.

'A cloud received Him out of their sight' (Acts 1:9). A cloud is a frequent biblical representation of the mystery and glory of God's presence, what was known as the Shekinah (Exodus 19:16; 24:15ff, etc.). Many have identified the cloud on the Mount of Transfiguration with God's presence (Luke 9:34). A cloud was a similarly appropriate symbol on the Mount of Olives for it was into the Father's immediate presence that Jesus was received. It conveyed the thought of His reception into glory. The One whom the disciples not long before had seen hanging on a tree between two thieves, they now saw taken up into heaven in great glory. As they had been witnesses of His Resurrection, so now they were witnesses of His Ascension. The mention of the cloud places no emphasis upon distance, only upon hiddenness.

Significantly Luke records, 'And they worshipped Him, and returned to Jerusalem with great joy' (24:52). When we recall the sorrow they showed at the Last Supper at every mention of His leaving them, we see the difference His Resurrection and Ascension made. They were now in no doubt about His identity as the Son of God. The Resurrection and Ascension were keys to the jigsaw putting everything Jesus had said and done into place. They knew their Lord to be worthy of their worship and the source of their joy (Luke 24:52, 53).

A message from heaven

The 'two men …in white apparel'—whom we may identify as angels—instructed the apostles that our Lord Jesus Christ's return will be after the pattern of His Ascension. Understandably the disciples initially stood amazed at the manner of their Lord's disappearance from their view. The two men in white who came to stand beside them asked, 'Men of Galilee, why do you stand gazing up into heaven? This same Jesus, who was taken up from you into heaven, will so come in like manner as you saw Him go into heaven' (Acts 1:11).

The angels explained the significance of the Ascension, and encouraged the disciples to see in it the anticipation they—and all God's people—

should have of Jesus' return. Taken up in a cloud (Acts 1:9), Jesus will come in the clouds (Daniel 7:13; Mark 13:26; 14:62; Revelation 1:7). Taken up in glory (1 Timothy 3:16), He will come in great glory (Matthew 16:27; 24:30; 25:31). Taken up physically into heaven, so He will physically return: 'Every eye will see Him, and they also who pierced Him. And all the tribes of the earth will mourn because of Him' (Revelation 1:7). Taken up on a precise day in human history, so He will return in human history on a literal day already fixed by God.

The Ascension was the conclusion of Jesus' bodily or physical presence in the world until that return. He signalled by it His final disappearance into that other realm that is now hidden from us—that realm where God's glory is perfectly revealed.

An act of power

The Ascension was an act of God's power. Significantly Mark, Luke (both in his gospel and the *Acts*) and Paul do not simply record that Jesus 'went up' but that He was 'received up into heaven' (Mark 16:19), 'carried up into heaven' (Luke 24:51), 'taken up' (Acts 1:2) and 'received up in glory' (1 Timothy 3:16). We do not have to look for a natural or scientific explanation. God, who made the world and the universe, who caused His Son to be conceived in the womb of the virgin Mary, and who raised Him from the dead on the third day, is the One who exalted Him. Crucified in weakness, Jesus now 'lives by the power of God' (2 Corinthians 13:4). Even as the only explanation of our Lord's Resurrection is God's Almighty power, so too is His Ascension—the two are inseparable. Writing about God's power to the Ephesians, Paul prays that they may know 'what is the exceeding greatness of His power toward us who believe, according to the working of His mighty power which He worked in Christ when He raised Him from the dead and seated Him at His right hand in the heavenly places, far above all principality and power and might and dominion, and every name that is named, not only in this age but also in that which is to come' (Ephesians 1:19-21).

The Ascension was essentially and uniquely God the Father's doing: He raised His Son and took Him to His right hand. 'I go to My Father,' the Lord Jesus explained to the disciples in the upper room (John

14:12,28; 16:17). 'I came forth from the Father and have come into the world. Again, I leave the world and go to the Father' (John 16:28). As the writer to the Hebrews expresses it, He has 'passed through the heavens' (Hebrews 4:14). The Ascension was His being taken up into heaven (Acts 1:2,9,10,11). Our Saviour is glorified in the Father's presence with the glory He had with Him before the world began (John 17:5).

After the Ascension the disciples returned to Jerusalem 'with great joy' and 'praising and blessing God' (Luke 24:52,53). They reflected the mood of Psalm 47:5: 'God has gone up with a shout, the LORD with the sound of a trumpet' even as Jesus had earlier promised they would, now they understood why their Lord had had to suffer before entering into His glory (Matthew 16:21; Luke 24:26).

A concluding proclamation of identity

From the beginning God the Father proclaimed the identity of His Son. Starting with Jesus' birth at Bethlehem, God announced through the angel, 'For there is born to you this day in the city of David, a Saviour, who is Christ the Lord' (Luke 2:11). Then Magi, wise men, from the east came, asking, 'Where is He who has been born King of the Jews?' and significantly when they found Him, they 'fell down and worshipped Him' (Matthew 2:2,11). The miracles Jesus performed were signs revealing and declaring who He was to those wanting to know the truth about Him. Finally, on the third day after the Crucifixion, God raised Him from the dead, and forty days afterwards received Him into heaven—a deliberate declaration of His identity.

In His early interview with Nicodemus Jesus said, 'No one has ascended to heaven but He who came down from heaven, that is, the Son of Man' (John 3:13). (Initially and superficially, this latter statement may seem to contradict what we understand happened with first Enoch and then Elijah. Genesis 5:24 records that 'Enoch walked with God; and he was not, for God took him.' The Bible gives more detail concerning Elijah's ascension. As Elijah and Elisha walked together, 'suddenly a chariot of fire appeared with horses of fire, and separated the two of them; and Elijah went up by a whirlwind into heaven' (2 Kings 2:11). We are able to recognise the superficial nature of the similarity between these two incidents and our Lord's

Ascension when we look carefully at the context of John 3:13. Jesus had just pointed out Nicodemus' ignorance not only of 'earthly' but also 'heavenly things' (3:12). He then carefully linked His Ascension with His having already come *from* heaven. As the Son of God Incarnate, His ascent to heaven could not have taken place without His descent first from heaven. In this He was, and is, unique. Jesus was declaring that apart from Him no one has been in heaven and then brought heavenly realities to this world. As the writer of Proverbs asks, 'Who has ascended into heaven, or descended?' (30:4). He is the unique link between heaven and earth. He alone therefore can reveal heavenly truth to men and women.)

Peter gave the right explanation and emphasis on the Day of Pentecost. Filled as he was with the Holy Spirit, he explained, 'David did not ascend into the heavens, but he says himself, "The LORD said to my Lord, 'Sit at My right hand, till I make Your enemies Your footstool.'" Therefore let all the house of Israel know assuredly that God has made this Jesus, whom you crucified, both Lord and Christ' (Acts 2:34-36). The Ascension adds its weight to the Resurrection by reversing, through God's own definitive verdict, the false verdict unbelieving men and women made on Jesus. As the hymn of praise in Philippians 2 puts it, 'God also has highly exalted Him and given Him the name which is above every name, that at the name of Jesus every knee should bow, of those in heaven, and of those on earth, and of those under the earth, and that every tongue should confess that Jesus Christ is Lord, to the glory of God the Father' (Philippians 2:9-11).

As the Resurrection marked out our Lord Jesus Christ as the Son of God (Romans 1:4), so the Ascension marked Him out as Lord (Philippians 2:9-11). The word 'Lord' is used over 6000 times in the Septuagint (the Greek translation of the Old Testament) for the name of God. Our Lord's Ascension, seen as His return to the Father, underlines the truth of His pre-existence before His human birth. Some who opposed His teaching and ministry chose to accuse Him of being an impostor. By raising Him from the dead, God the Father put the record straight and affirmed, 'This is my Son'. By exalting Him to His right hand, God the Father declared Him 'Lord', worthy of worship as God.

A fundamental statement of the early Church, probably part of an early Christian hymn, was: 'And without controversy great is the mystery of godliness: God was manifested in the flesh, justified in the Spirit, seen by angels, preached among the Gentiles, believed on in the world, received up in glory' (1 Timothy 3:16).

A sign of completion

When a new bridge is completed, or a major highway, authorities lay on a celebration. When building work is completed according to the contract, we sign completion certificates. Signs of a finished task are part of everyday life. The Ascension was a mark of achievement. As the Catechism of the Church of Geneva (1541) puts it, 'For after he had performed all the things which the Father had given Him to do, and which were for our salvation, there was no need of His continuing longer on earth' *(Calvin's Tracts and Treatises, Vol. II, p.48)*.

Return to the Father

The Ascension signalled Jesus' return to the Father. He had come from the Father, and it was to the Father that He returned. Gospel writer John introduces his unique account of our Lord's washing the disciples' feet with the words, 'Jesus knew that His hour had come that He should depart from this world to the Father' (John 13:1).

Jesus' return to the Father was a joyful prospect constantly before Him throughout His ministry, and not least when He anticipated the agonies of the Cross. To Jews who sent Temple guards to arrest Him, He said, 'I shall be with you a little while longer, and then I go to Him who sent Me. You will seek Me and not find Me, and where I am you cannot come' (John 7:33,34). To grieving disciples in the upper room, He said, 'You have heard Me say to you, "I am going away and coming back to you." If you loved Me, you would rejoice because I said, "I am going to the Father"' (John 14:28). 'Now I go away to Him who sent Me' (John 16:5).

The great cost of the Incarnation to the Son of God was His leaving 'the bosom of the Father' (John 1:18). The closeness of the Father and the Son cannot be expressed in human language. The cost of complete separation from the Father on the Cross as He became sin for His people was an even greater price. That devastating and indescribable experience is now past and complete. The Lord Jesus is again 'in the bosom of the Father'.

Chapter 4

Raised to ascend

The Ascension was the necessary completion of our Lord Jesus Christ's work after His Death and Resurrection. Luke records that 'when the time had come for Him to be received up, that He steadfastly set His face to go to Jerusalem' (Luke 9:51). Luke clearly understood Jesus' Ascension to be as essential to the divine programme as Jesus' Death and Resurrection were. He died and was raised *in order to ascend*. The Resurrection and the Ascension were one continuous movement in the apostolic preaching, and together they constituted His exaltation.

Peter declared at Pentecost, 'This Jesus God has raised up, of which we are all witnesses. Therefore being exalted to the right hand of God, and having received from the Father the promise of the Holy Spirit, He poured out this which you now see and hear' (Acts 2:32,33). He was 'raised' to be 'exalted'. Years later Peter wrote about Jesus' Resurrection. He immediately followed his reference to it with the statement that Jesus 'has gone into heaven and is at the right hand of God, angels and authorities and powers having been made subject to Him' (1 Peter 3:21,22). He automatically linked the Resurrection with the Ascension. Paul does the same (Ephesians 1:19-21).

The Death and Resurrection of Jesus must not be separated from His Ascension, for the last was equally vital to His work for us. His Death and Resurrection could not have their full effect until He ascended to His Father, with His work of atonement complete (Hebrews 4:14).

Powerful symbols of the Father's acceptance

God the Father's acceptance of His Son into glory decisively declared His acceptance of our Lord Jesus Christ's sacrifice for our sins. While the sacrifice itself took place on earth, His entrance into glory gave the clear message of its acceptance in heaven. Two simple yet profound symbols are used: 'sitting' and 'the right hand of God'. Symbols are the nearest we can get to understanding truths beyond our comprehension until we witness their reality. These two pictures powerfully present spiritual truth.

First, we consider the symbol of sitting. The writer to the Hebrews delights in the simple sentence 'He sat down'. Chapter One opens with the glorious declaration that God has spoken to us by His Son. There then follow six subordinate clauses concerning Jesus: first, 'whom He has appointed heir of all things'; second, 'through whom also He made the worlds'; third, who is 'the brightness of His glory'; fourth, 'the express image of His person'; fifth, 'upholding all things by the word of His power'; sixth, 'when He had by Himself purged our sins'—and then we arrive at the climax—'sat down at the right hand of the Majesty on high' (1:3). He later writes of Jesus as being 'seated at the right hand of the throne of the Majesty in the heavens' (8:1; cf. 10:12; 12:2). The Lord Jesus Himself used the symbol in addressing the church at Laodicea. He promises, 'To him who overcomes I will grant to sit with Me on My throne, as I also overcame and sat down with My Father on His throne' (Revelation 3:21). The tense in each case is the aorist. The chief function of that tense is to indicate an instantaneous action, no matter whether present, future or past, and to underline 'the once for all' nature of whatever is described.

The symbolism is important. Imagine our visiting either the Tabernacle or the Temple. One feature would have been conspicuous: we would have seen sacrifices repeated daily by the priests. Their work was always incomplete, and they never sat down while they were carrying out their ministry. Think of the hundreds and thousands of priests throughout all the centuries preceding Jesus' sacrifice upon the Cross. None ever sat in God's Holy Place. Luke tells of John the Baptist's father, Zechariah, who served as a priest before God. 'According to the custom of the priesthood, his lot fell to burn incense when he went into the temple of the Lord' (Luke 1:9). One thing Zechariah never did, or thought of doing, was to sit down in the Lord's sanctuary. There were no seats either in the Tabernacle or Temple furniture.

As an outward sign that their work was never finished, the priests always stood in their service. The Lord set apart the tribe of Levi to carry the ark of the covenant of the Lord, the instruction was that they were 'to stand before the LORD to minister to Him' (Deuteronomy 10:8). Jesus, however, offered one sacrifice for sins for ever—a perfect sacrifice—and then sat down. His sitting down was equivalent to saying 'Mission accomplished'! His atoning sacrifice for our sins is gloriously complete.

In everyday life, sitting suggests completion. A busy mother's family may ask her, 'When are you going to sit down?' Her answer may be, 'When I have finished what I need to do!' Our Saviour's sitting signifies what we describe as 'the finished work of Christ'. His sacrifice was final, conclusive and for ever. He does not even need to offer that sacrifice continually to God. His sitting declares the Father's complete satisfaction with what Jesus perfectly accomplished at Calvary. By seating His Son at His right hand, the Father was declaring, as at His Son's baptism and Transfiguration, 'This is My beloved Son, in whom I am well pleased' (Matthew 3:17; 17:5).

Second, we consider the symbol of the right hand of God. Separating the two pictures is difficult. Used frequently, the truths they represent merge into one another. However, each is worthy of consideration. Our Saviour's sitting at the right hand of God is a New Testament emphasis (Acts 2:33; 5:31; Ephesians 1:20; Colossians 3:1; Hebrews 1:3; 8:1; 10:12; 12:2; 1 Peter 3:22). It arises from God the Father's promise, recorded in Psalm 110:1, 'Sit at My right hand, till I make Your enemies Your footstool.'

Where the Lord Jesus sat down is as important as the fact that He did sit down: He sat down at the Father's right hand. An essential truth arises from this, identical to what we highlighted regarding the symbol of sitting. The right hand of God is the place of acceptance. Unless God had been satisfied with the work of atonement, there could have been no salvation. Our Lord's presence 'at the right hand of the Majesty on high' (Hebrews 1:3) proclaims the Father's recognition and satisfaction with His Son's work on the Cross.

Besides expressing the Father's acceptance, the Son's sitting at His right hand symbolises too His elevation to the highest possible position of honour. Sitting at the Father's right hand is a picture taken from the world of kings, princes and rulers. For example, we are told that when Bathsheba went to speak to King Solomon on behalf of Adonijah 'the king rose up to meet her and bowed down to her, and sat down on his throne and had a throne set for the king's mother; so she sat at his right hand' (1 Kings 2:19). This action showed Bathsheba's influence, and, significantly, she then went on to make a request of the king. The right hand of God indicates our Saviour's influence in that He has continual access to the Father.

The Catechism of the Church of Geneva (1541) asks, 'In what sense do you say that He "sitteth on the right of the Father?"' The answer then given, springs from Matthew 28:18; 'These words mean that the Father bestowed upon Him the dominion of heaven and earth, so that He governs all things' (*Calvin's Tracts and Treatises, Vol. II*, p.49). Sovereignty (Psalm 110:2; Zechariah 6:12f), authority (Psalm 48:10; 77:10) and power (Psalm 17:7; 18:35; 20:6; 21:8; 60:5; 74:11; 98:1; 118:15f; Isaiah 48:13; 62:8) are clearly conveyed by this picture.

Jesus' exaltation and our being declared 'Not guilty' in the court of heaven

Both symbols point to our Lord's unique position at the Father's side and the Father's full acceptance of the Son's single sacrifice for sins for all time. 'Him God has exalted to His right hand to be Prince and Saviour, to give repentance to Israel and forgiveness of sins' (Acts 5:31).

Each aspect of our Saviour's work has the utmost relevance to us. His Death removed the guilt of our sin. His Resurrection declared the destruction of the power of sin, and not least the abolition of sin's destructive power with regard to death (2 Timothy 1:10). His Ascension assures us that He has removed the separation from God that sin caused. He has entered God's presence for us, and God accepts us in Him. As John Calvin's Catechism of the Church of Geneva again puts it, 'For inasmuch as Christ entered heaven in our name, just as He had come down to earth on our account, He also opened up access for us, so that the door, previously shut because of sin, is now open' (*Calvin's Tracts and Treatises, Vol.II*, p. 48).

We are encouraged to picture ourselves in a law court. The court is that of heaven, the final tribunal before which all men and women must ultimately appear and answer. 'Who shall bring a charge against God's elect?' Paul asks in Romans 8. He replies, 'It is God who justifies. Who is he who condemns? It is Christ who died, and furthermore is also risen, who is even at the right hand of God, who also makes intercession for us. Who shall separate us from the love of Christ?' (Romans 8:33-35).

The forgiveness of our sins and our acceptance with God, through our union with Christ, are unassailable. Who dares to accuse those whom God has chosen and justified (Romans 8:33)? Satan, the accuser of God's people, may dare to do so, but no accusation can stand for a moment against them. The Judge Himself declares us free from sin (Romans 8:33)! Who then is in a position to condemn us? Only Christ, into whose hands the Father has committed all authority to judge men and women, and He died for us, rose for us, ascended for us, reigns in power for us, and prays for us! He ascended into heaven to plead our cause at God's right hand. In the face of such assurances, what is there left to say? To take up Paul's words again, 'If God is for us, who can be against us?' (Romans 8:31). Our position in the Lord Jesus Christ is eternally secure!

John Bunyan, in his book *Grace Abounding*, describes how forcefully this truth came to him. 'But one day, as I was passing in the field, and that too with some dashes on my conscience, fearing lest yet all was not right, suddenly this sentence fell upon my soul, "Thy righteousness is in heaven"; and me thought withal, I saw, with the eyes of my soul, Jesus Christ at God's right hand; there, I say, is my righteousness, so that wherever I was, or whatever I was a-doing, God could not say of me, he wants (*i.e. lacks*) my righteousness, for that was just before Him. I also saw, moreover, that it was not my good frame of heart that made my righteousness better, nor yet my bad frame that made my righteousness worse; for my righteousness was Jesus Christ Himself, the same yesterday, and today, and forever.'

John Flavel, the seventeenth century Puritan writer, argues in a similar vein. 'If Christ had not ascended, how could we have been satisfied that His payment on the Cross made full satisfaction to God, and that now God has no more bills to bring in against us?'

Our Lord's sitting at the right hand of the Father provides grounds for the greatest possible peace in spite of our guilty consciences, and all that they may tell us to our discredit. Little wonder that Christians have expressed this great truth in praise and song!

When Satan tempts me to despair,
And tells me of the guilt within,
Upward I look, and see Him there
Who made an end of all my sin.

Because the sinless Saviour died,
My guilty soul is counted free;
For God, the Just, is satisfied
To look on Him and pardon me.
(Charitee Lees Bancroft)

No condemnation now I dread;
Jesus and all in Him, is mine!
Alive in Him, my living Head,
And clothed in righteousness divine,
Bold I approach the eternal throne
And claim the crown through Christ my own.
(Charles Wesley)

A truth to explore further

Our Saviour's sitting at the right hand of God cannot be separated from the glorious prospect of His return. He sits because He waits; He rests until His enemies are subdued (Hebrews 10:13). While His sitting reminds us that His coming again was not immediate upon His Ascension, it also keeps alive in our thoughts that this is His people's hope and assurance for the future. That is a subject to which we must return.

The Man in Glory

A ll truth is valuable, but some truths are particularly significant and meaningful. One such is the description of our Lord Jesus Christ as 'the Man in glory'. It is not a biblical title but it sums up biblical truth. In his letter to the Colossians, Paul affirms of our Lord Jesus Christ, 'In Him dwells all the fullness of the Godhead bodily' (Colossians 2:9). His use of the present tense is important, since he was writing a number of years after the Ascension. The Greek present tense may be used, as a perfect tense in that language is normally used, in order to express the continuance in the present of a state begun in the past. Its employment here is telling. All Deity lives in 'the Man in glory'—our Ascended Lord Jesus—as it was embodied in the Incarnation. He is not only God, but God clothed in our nature. Our Lord's humanity continues to give meaning and significance to His heavenly existence. In other words, the Lord Jesus did not put off His humanity in assuming His rightful place in glory. In becoming man—genuinely human, apart from sin—for the sake of our salvation, the Lord Jesus, the Second Person of the Trinity, became what He never was before. He remains so forever.

A new experience for our Saviour's humanity

Our Lord's visible ascent from earth to heaven was in a manner appropriate to His human nature. He was exalted to the place in the universe that He laid aside when He humbled Himself to take upon Himself our humanity. Paul appropriately asks in Ephesians 4:9,10: '(Now this, "*He ascended*"— what does it mean but that He also first descended into the lower parts of the earth? He who descended is also the One who ascended far above all the heavens, that He might fill all things.)'

Something startlingly new and significant happened at our Lord's Ascension. He took His human body—our humanity—with Him to heaven. As Rabbi Duncan expressed it, 'The dust of the earth is on the Throne of the universe.' While He had always been with the Father before His Incarnation, enjoying perfect fellowship with Him, He had not before been in heaven as the Word made flesh. This was a completely new experience for Him as our Emmanuel, God incarnate for us.

Our Lord Jesus possesses in heaven the same body in its human nature as He had on earth. In the Book of Revelation He appears as 'a Lamb as though it had been slain' (Revelation 5:6). He retains the body He offered for us when He bore our sins on the Cross. During His earthly ministry Jesus' body was in a state of humiliation, in that it was subject to the limitations our human bodies know, including death. This was followed by a state of resurrection during the forty days. His body was the same but different. It was the same in that He could eat with His disciples (Luke 24:41-43) and yet different in that, for example, He could suddenly stand among them when the doors were locked (John 20:19). At His Ascension His body passed into its glorified state. We are not in a position to understand the wonders of this glorified state now. However, 'we know that when He is revealed, we shall be like Him, for we shall see Him as He is' (1 John 3:2). Writing on the Lord's Supper, John Calvin said, 'The body of our Lord in heaven [is] the same as that which He had on earth. ... Scripture everywhere teaches us, that, as the Lord on earth took humanity, so He has exalted it to heaven, withdrawing it from mortal condition, but not changing its nature' (Calvin: *Short Treatise on the Lord's Supper, Tracts II*, p. 187). Elsewhere Calvin writes, 'The whole of Scripture proclaims that Christ now lives His glorious life in our flesh, just as surely as it was in our flesh that He once suffered ...' (On 2 Corinthians 5:16). The *Westminster Shorter Catechism* affirms, Christ 'who, being the eternal Son of God, became man, and so was, and continueth to be, God and man in two distinct natures, and one person, for ever.' Our Lord's Ascension into heaven in His human nature is a fundamental of the Christian faith.

The occasion of our Saviour's glorification

When our Lord Jesus carried His humanity back to heaven, He was highly exalted and glorified in doing so. 'God ... glorified His Servant Jesus' was the apostolic testimony (Acts 3:13). The Father has honoured Him with the highest standing as the Word made flesh returned to heaven. The title 'Servant' in the apostolic testimony is significant because it relates specifically to our Lord's Incarnation and saving work. It is as the Servant—the Messiah—that the Father has glorified Him.

Our Lord's position now is different from what it was before His Incarnation. At His Ascension He resumed His position of glory. He prayed, for example, in what we call His high-priestly prayer in John 17, 'And now, O Father, glorify Me together with Yourself, with the glory which I had with You before the world was' (17:5). Eternally divine, His essential glory has not increased. Nothing can be added to divine perfection. His Ascension, however, revealed His 'official glory' as the triumphant Servant of the Lord. He came into the world to be the Saviour, the one Mediator between God and man. During His time in this world, however, He was not appreciated by those He came to save. But now His believing people delight to recognise the glorious office He holds as the exalted Emmanuel. The Church is now a unique instrument to proclaim and express His glory. His people delight to honour Him. His unique glory is that of the obedient suffering Servant of the Lord who perfectly fulfilled the Father's will in the divine plan of salvation.

The powerful truth of our Saviour's sympathy

To become our great High Priest and Saviour, the Lord Jesus participated in our nature of flesh and blood (Hebrews 2:14-18). He was made like us in every way, apart from sin, so that He might become a merciful and faithful High Priest. He experienced life in a human body (Hebrews 2:14). He was made perfect through the experience of suffering: 'Though He was a Son, yet He learned obedience by the things which He suffered' (Hebrews 5:8). We may feel rather uncomfortable at first with such an expression. But the fact that it is used shows how clearly the writer perceived the genuineness of our Lord's humanity. It was because he was absolutely sure of it that he could speak of it in this way.

The writer to the Hebrews' use of the word 'obedience' does not imply that our Lord was ever rebellious or disobedient. Rather it emphasises that while He always possessed the disposition to obey, He could possess the virtue of obedience only as that disposition was put to the test. The particular reference is to our Lord's agony in the Garden. We cannot enter into the sufferings of His soul as He contemplated the Cross. Being sinless, the contemplation of bearing the sin of the whole world upon Him was awesome, and His sweat was as great drops of blood. It was by such severe testing that our Lord was 'perfected' (9)—another daring phrase. This does not imply that our Lord was previously imperfect, and that He was brought out of a state of imperfection. 'There is the perfection of the bud of the rose which is not the same as the perfection of the flower into which in course of time it grows. The word "made perfect" has about it the idea of reaching one's proper end or aim ...' (Leon Morris). We get the better sense if we substitute the word 'complete'. It was by such testing that our Lord was made 'complete' in that thereby He demonstrated that He possessed every necessary qualification to be the High Priest—and the perfect sacrifice—we need. Our Lord always possessed the disposition of obedience, as we have said, but for Him to possess the virtue of obedience, testing was necessary—and He was proved perfect! Genuinely man, He was tempted in every way as we are (Hebrews 4:15). He prayed with loud cries and tears (Hebrews 5:7).

As a wonderful consequence of our Lord's taking His glorified humanity into heaven, 'we do not have a High Priest who cannot sympathise with our weaknesses, but was in all points tempted as we are, yet without sin' (Hebrews 4:15). This assurance makes even more meaningful the knowledge that the Lord Jesus treats us as family, as brothers and sisters (Psalm 22:22; Hebrews 2:11,12). He totally identifies Himself with us. He knows what we need, and how we feel. His perfect sensitivity and awareness of our situation always leads to the most appropriate action on our behalf. He is utterly faithful to us and our interests.

Our Saviour's 'unfinished' work in heaven is His keeping, helping, and perfecting us until our sanctification is complete, as it will be when we arrive where He now is. As Richard Sibbes, the sixteenth century Puritan, quoting Hebrews 5:1, put it, 'Our God and our man, our God-man is ascended unto the high court of heaven, to His and our God, clothed with our nature. Is there any more able and willing to plead our cause, or to whom we may trust business with, than He, who is in "heaven, for all things for us, appertaining to God"?'

Our Lord's retention of His humanity makes even more wonderful and potent His ability to sympathise in all our moments of human desperation whether on account of weakness, suffering or difficulty. I cannot help but wonder what it was that identified the Lord Jesus to Stephen as he looked up to heaven at the time of his martyrdom. Filled with the Holy Spirit, it was clearly the Spirit who helped him to make that identification. But was it the marks of the Crucifixion that Stephen saw in his glorified Lord, that made him appreciate and rejoice in his Master's unique ability to sympathise with him and to help him through his ordeal?

The assurance of our own future human glorification

The Ascension was not only the exaltation of our Lord Jesus as man, but also the elevation of our humanity in Him. The Lord Jesus has carried our nature to the right hand of the Father. As we think of our own physical nature of flesh and bones present there in our Lord Jesus, we have the glorious prospect of our bodies being there too. Our citizenship as believers is already in heaven. 'From which we also eagerly wait for the Saviour, the Lord Jesus Christ, who will transform our lowly body that it may be conformed to His glorious body, according to the working by which He is able even to subdue all things to Himself' (Philippians 3:20,21). Behind this glorious assurance is the work of our Lord Jesus Christ as the last Adam. He became what the first Adam was intended to be. He is the new man, the beginning of God's new creation. In the Lord Jesus we exchange the perishable for the imperishable, and the mortal for immortality (1 Corinthians 15:52-54). 'And as we have borne the image of the man of dust, we shall also bear the image of the heavenly Man' (1 Corinthians 15:49).

Quoting Genesis 3:19, Gregory the Great (540-604) saw the Ascension as a cause for great joy on this account, 'For that nature, to whom it was said, "Dust you are and to dust you will return", has entered into heaven today.' The Lord Jesus both rose and ascended as the first-fruits of a great harvest. Little wonder Augustine (354-430) said, 'My thoughts, and the deepest places of my soul are torn with every kind of tumult until the day when I shall be purified and melted in the fire of Your love, and wholly joined to You.'

A reminder of the physical nature of our Lord's return

Isidore, Archbishop of Seville in the sixth century, contributed much to the life of the Church by his writings. In one of his books, he wrote of Ascension Day, 'This festival is celebrated throughout the course of the years in order that the manhood of the assumed flesh ascending to the right hand of the Father might be recalled, whose body we believe to be in heaven, in such fashion as when He ascended and the angel's voice proclaiming it, saying: "He shall so come in like manner as ye beheld him going into heaven", i.e. with the same form and substance of flesh, to which flesh He truly gave immortality and did not withdraw its nature' (*De Ecclesiasticae Officiis*).

The Book of Revelation exhorts us, 'Behold, He is coming with clouds, and every eye will see Him' (Revelation 1:7). We shall return later to this subject when we consider our Lord's present waiting.

A strong source of strength and comfort

The Scottish paraphrase, *Where high the heavenly temple stands* has three telling verses that dwell upon our Lord's retained humanity:

Though now ascended up on high,
He bends on earth a brother's eye;
Partaker of the human name,
He knows the frailty of our frame.

Our fellow-sufferer yet retains
A fellow-feeling of our pains,
And still remembers in the skies
His tears, His agonies and cries.

In every pang that rends the heart,
The Man of Sorrows had a part;
He sympathises with our grief,
And to the sufferer sends relief.
(Scottish Paraphrases No. 58, 1781. From Hebrews 4:14-end.)

Priest, Intercessor and Advocate

'Finished' is a word that gloriously describes the Lord Jesus Christ's saving work on the Cross. It tells us that His sacrifice for our sins is complete and that nothing may be added to it. At the same time, and not in conflict with that fundamental of the Christian faith, the Bible teaches that the Lord Jesus has a continuing work on behalf of His people, and it is to this that we now turn our attention.

His priesthood

If we have to choose the most fundamental part of our Lord's present ministry, it must be His priesthood. It is His foundation office, and more fundamental to our salvation than His office as King.

The idea of priesthood is not so familiar to us as it was to first century Christians. Jews in particular were accustomed to it. The Letter to the Hebrews concentrates upon this aspect of our Lord Jesus' saving work. The Jewish Christians, to whom it was addressed, appreciated the need for priests or intermediaries between God and sinful men and women. Abandoning dependence upon human priesthood in their approach to God had been difficult for some of them.

Because of our unfamiliarity with the idea of priesthood, we may fail to value that of our Lord Jesus Christ as we ought. The writer to the Hebrews suggests that the appreciation of our Saviour's priesthood has much to do with our spiritual maturity or immaturity (Hebrews 6:1; 10:1). He describes teaching about it as 'solid food' in contrast to 'milk' (Hebrews 5:11-14).

Two basic qualifications were necessary for a priest in the Old Testament. First, he had to possess the ability to sympathise with those he represented. Second, he had to be divinely appointed to office (Hebrews 5:1-4). Our Lord Jesus uniquely fulfils both qualifications. As we saw earlier, Psalm 110:4 refers to His priestly rule: 'The LORD has sworn and will not relent, "You are a priest for ever according to the order of Melchizedek."' Without the Lord Jesus' priesthood there would be no salvation for us—it is as simple as that! Without His continuing priesthood, we would be lost, for we constantly make mistakes, sin and fall into error. Through our great High Priest there is always mercy for us at God's throne.

A permanent priesthood

The New Testament emphasises that the Lord Jesus lives *for ever* as our Priest. We can see at once how totally different His priesthood is therefore from any other. Throughout Israel's history countless Jewish priests had this in common—they all died, and when they died their priesthood ended. The Lord Jesus, however, lives 'according to the power of an endless life' (Hebrews 7:16). He took on the devil who holds the power of death, and death could not hold Him (Hebrews 2:14,15).

The Lord Jesus is the Living One, who was dead, and is alive for ever and ever (Revelation 1:18). He is the 'I AM'—the Self-Existent One. He spoke of Himself as the Bread of Life (John 6:35), the Light of the world (John 8:12; 9:5), the Door of the sheep (John 10:7), the Good Shepherd (John 10:11,14), the Resurrection and the Life (John 11:25), the Way, the Truth, the Life (John 14:6), and the True Vine (John 15:1). He significantly prefaced each title with the words 'I AM'. Discerning Jews recognised the use of the divine name, revealed to Moses (Exodus 3:14f), meaning 'I will be who or what I will be'. Because Jesus lives for ever, He has a permanent priesthood (Hebrews 7:24).

A totally different priesthood

We need to underline what our Lord Jesus Christ's priesthood does not mean as well as what it does. At His Ascension He entered upon His work as a royal priest 'at the right hand of the throne of the Majesty in the heavens' (Hebrews 8:1), no longer needing to offer atoning sacrifice to God.

That He, the priest, should be upon the throne underlines the fact that His priesthood is different from any other (Hebrews 12:2; Revelation 3:21). The Ascension was not part of His atoning work. Rather it was His enthronement as the High Priest, whose work of making propitiation for our sins was already complete. He did not offer His glorified body to God, but His physical body through death at Calvary, the body of flesh and blood in which He took our sins upon Him as a propitiatory sacrifice.

His Ascension to be our Priest does not mean that He continually offers a sacrifice for our sins. Everywhere in the New Testament the stress is upon the *once-and-for-all* nature of His atoning sacrifice. The Letter to the Hebrews gives this particular emphasis. That sacrifice took place uniquely once. It was so perfect and sufficient that it *finally* dealt with the problem of human guilt. As a result, all who believe on the Son of God receive complete forgiveness and are eternally secure. Our attention is drawn to this assurance. Unlike the other high priests, He 'does not need daily … to offer up sacrifices, first for His own sins and then for the people's, for this He did once for all when He offered up Himself' (Hebrews 7:27). His sitting down at the Father's right hand witnesses to the 'once-for-all' character of His atoning sacrifice (Hebrews 1:3; 8:1). 'But this Man, after He had offered one sacrifice for sins for ever, sat down at the right hand of God' (Hebrews 10:12).

Any suggestion that the Lord Jesus needs to plead continually His death before His Father is out of place. The Father is not to be thought of as in some way reluctant to have mercy upon men and women. Such an idea is totally inappropriate because the initiative in the whole plan of salvation was the Father's. As John 3:16 so clearly puts it, 'For God (*that is, the Father*) so loved the world that He gave His only begotten Son.' It was the Father who sent the Son (1 John 4:9,10,14). It was the Father who determined the sacrifice that would be sufficient for the sins of the whole world. It was the Father who raised His Son, and took Him to His own right hand to underscore His acceptance of us in Him.

So our Lord Jesus does not have to plead His sacrifice. He does not need to offer Himself afresh to the Father, or to re-present His sacrifice to Him. Our Lord's position in heaven, glorified and exalted, is God's guarantee of the eternal effectiveness of His Son's finished work. This explains the emphasis in Hebrews that we should fix our eyes upon Jesus (Hebrews 3:1; 12:2). That is another way of saying that we should focus upon *who* He is, *what* He has done for us, and *where* He now is. If we fix our eyes upon ourselves, we will fall into a common snare of fallen human nature as it thinks about a relationship with God, and we will say, '*Do*.' If we fix them upon Jesus, we will declare '*Done*'! Our Lord's presence with the Father is the secret of our peace, the assurance of our access to God, and the guarantee of our permanent relationship to Him (Hebrews 10:19-22).

Significantly, when our Lord Jesus ascended, He gave 'some to be apostles, some prophets, some evangelists, and some pastors and teachers' (Ephesians 4:11), but none to be priests! In Him we have the High Priest who meets all our need (Hebrews 7:26; 8:1). He makes His appearance before God as High Priest *for us* (Hebrews 9:24). Those two words 'for us' give great comfort and assurance. All that the Lord Jesus does as Priest is *for* His people. When we draw near to God, it is not with any reliance whatsoever upon our works and merits, but entirely upon Jesus' work for us. It is because He is our perfect great High Priest that we have become spiritual priests, able to approach God at any time through Him.

Our priest's intercession

The New Testament speaks twice of Jesus' intercession for His people. In Romans 8 Paul declares, 'It is Christ who died, and furthermore is also risen, who is even at the right hand of God, who also makes intercession for us' (verse 34). In Hebrews 7:25, an often quoted verse, we read 'He ever lives to make intercession' for us. Although we frequently refer to this aspect of Jesus' work, and rightly so as a ground of great comfort, we seldom explain it. As a result, there are dangers of defective understanding of what He now does. There is no doubt about its importance, for as John Owen (1616-1683) declares, 'The actual intercession of Christ in heaven ... is a fundamental article of our faith, and a principal foundation of the church's consolation ... it compriseth the whole care and all the actings of Christ, as our high priest, with God in the behalf of the Church' (Owen, *Works XXII*, p. 538).

We need to be clear about the precise nature of this intercession. Does it mean that our Lord Jesus pleads vocally with the Father? This has been a matter of debate throughout church history. Gregory the Great raised it in the sixth century, and at the time of the Reformation different views separated the Lutheran and Reformed leaders. Lutheran leaders regarded the intercession as consisting literally in the offering of petitions. Reformed leaders, like John Calvin, however, interpreted the intercession as real but not oral or vocal. They saw it as consisting of our Lord Jesus Christ's presence at the Father's right hand, and not a matter of vocal supplication. Any idea of the Lord Jesus needing to plead vocally with the Father is inappropriate. God the Father is not an unwilling giver of benefits to those He has redeemed by the blood of His Son. The Son does not need to ask the Father to be gracious. Nowhere in the Bible is Jesus' intercession associated with the pleading of His sacrifice.

The proper conclusion seems to be that our Lord Jesus Christ's most powerful intercession for us is His presence at the Father's right hand, quite apart from what He asks the Father for us. His intercession is not vocal by means of entreaties, but certain and real by the merits of His blood (His eternal sacrifice) and by being at the throne of the Father. John's vision of heaven in the Book of Revelation is meaningful: 'And I looked, and behold, in the midst of the throne and of the four living creatures, and in the midst of the elders, stood a Lamb *as though it had been slain*' (Revelation 5:6). That is how the Father, the angels and His people always see our Lord in heaven.

Helps to understanding our Lord's intercession for us

We have to wrestle to put this truth of our Lord's intercession into human language that is neither ambiguous nor misleading. Four things may help us: first, the example of the High Priest in the Old Testament; second, an illustration from the life of David; third, the meaning of the verb 'intercede', and, fourth, the significance of prayer in Jesus' name. It is worth working hard to understand it for it is rich in its fruits.

First, the example of the High Priest in the Old Testament helps us to understand the nature of our Lord's intercession. The High Priest was distinctive because of his special garments intended 'for glory and for beauty' (Exodus 28:2). This was not on his own account but because of the One he represented and served. A crucial part of his dress was his breast-plate in which were mounted twelve precious stones in four rows. The precious stones were engraved with the names of the twelve tribes. They pointed to his function as representative of his people, especially as he made atonement for their sins. God's instruction was, 'And the stones shall have the names of the sons of Israel, twelve according to their names, like the engravings of a signet, each one with its own name; they shall be according to the twelve tribes' (Exodus 28:21).

In God the Father's infinite mercy and grace, He has chosen so to unite us to His Son that we are, among other privileges, both His Son's body and bride. As the High Priest had the names of the twelve tribes in precious stones written on his breastplate (Exodus 28:21,30), so our Lord Jesus Christ, our great High Priest, has the names of all His people in His heart, to present them always to God. As He appears before God, so the Church also appears before God in our Saviour's heart. All His desires for us—illustrated by those requests He vocally expressed in John 17—are constantly before the Father, because between them is perfect spiritual communion, a communion that does not require words for its expression. As by faith we see our Lord in the Father's presence, so we may see ourselves and our interests there too, for we are in His heart.

Second, an illustration from David's life helps to interpret our Lord's intercession. All illustrations of spiritual truth tend to fail to parallel exactly what we try to picture, but they may act as windows for glimpses of truth. We go back to the time of King David and the circumstances of the family and household of Mephibosheth. Mephibosheth was the son of Jonathan and grandson of King Saul.

Jonathan and David, the closest of friends, had sworn friendship with one another in the name of the Lord, a friendship to extend to their respective families (1 Samuel 20:42). Mephibosheth was only five years old when his father and grandfather died. As his nurse had picked him up to flee for his safety, he fell and became crippled. He, his family and his servants were in constant peril because they were seen as strong contenders for the succession to the throne. Many would have argued that on the grounds of political expediency Mephibosheth and his family should have been exterminated by David. Yet something happened that removed all immediate possibility of that, and the removal of fear.

David, out of love for his best friend Jonathan, discovered that Mephibosheth, the crippled son of Jonathan, was alive. Mephibosheth was brought before him. 'Do not fear, for I will surely show you kindness for Jonathan your father's sake, and will restore to you all the land of Saul your grandfather; and you shall eat bread at my table continually' (2 Samuel 9:7).

David's action transformed not only Mephibosheth's situation but that of his family too. His son and family could go about in peace, knowing all was well. That assurance came about because of *where* Mephibosheth was. His attendance at the king's table was a guarantee and symbol of their security. His physical presence there day by day was a reminder of all David had pledged. Mephibosheth did not have to plead the cause of his family and servants. His home and presence in the king's company, at the king's initiative, was enough. So it is for us—in greater measure still—regarding our Lord's position at God's right hand.

In his commentary on Hebrews, Bishop Westcott says of our Lord Jesus, 'His glorified humanity is the eternal pledge of the absolute efficacy of His accomplished work. He pleads, as older writers truly expressed the thought, by His presence on the Father's throne' (B.F. Westcott: *Hebrews*, p. 230). H.B. Swete, in his book, *The Ascended Christ*, agrees, 'The intercession of the Ascended Christ is not a prayer but a life. ... Our Lord's life in Heaven is His prayer.' As Calvin put it, 'Christ's intercession is the continual application of His death to our salvation' (Quoted by John Stott: *The Epistles of John*, p.82).

Third, the actual meaning of the word translated 'intercede' casts significant light on the way in which we are to interpret it. Where in English we always use a word in the same way, in another language the equivalent word may have more than one meaning, as happens here. While used of straightforward interceding for others, the Greek word used— *entunchano*—also bears the equal sense of *looking after someone's interests*. It suggests conferring or brooding over the interests of others. This is plainly true of our Lord's present activity as our High Priest. With mercy, compassion, love and tenderness, He cares for us and our best interests, and sends all the supplies of grace and help from heaven we need. The love He had for us when He laid down His life for us, is the love He has now, and will continue to have for all eternity. His perfect knowledge of our need is matched by His perfect acting on our behalf because of that knowledge. Chrysostom (c.344/354-407), bishop of Constantinople, spoke of our Lord's intercession as simply a way of expressing the warmth and strength of our Saviour's love for us. That interpretation fits this meaning of the Greek word 'intercede' as to 'look after the interests of'.

Fourth, our Lord's intercession has something to do with our prayers, offered in His Name. A wonder of our relationship to God our heavenly Father is that we may come to Him anytime and anywhere, but always in the Name of Jesus, our great High Priest. Whatever may be the significance in Revelation 5:8 of the reference to the 'golden bowls full of incense, which are the prayers of the saints', it is linked with the profound truth that the Lamb has made them kings and priests to God (Revelation 5:10). We rightly conclude our prayers with the words 'in the name of Jesus' or 'through Jesus Christ our Lord'. These expressions are not meaningless formulae; rather, they express a profound truth. While Jesus was in His physical body in the world, His principal purpose was to glorify the Father. We, as His Church, are His body, the body through which He now works in the world. His purpose has not changed. He gives to His body that objective of glorifying the Father as the main goal of Spirit-guided prayers (John 14:13,14). Where that is the object, the Lord Jesus intercedes for us by offering our prayers as His own.

Our Lord Jesus offers our prayers to the Father, and His own approval of them, as the Spirit within us helps us to pray in accord with God's will. As we pray, we have One who works with us on earth—the Holy Spirit—and One who works with us in heaven—our High Priest. The prayers the Spirit inspires, and even the desires we cannot put into words, are presented by Him to our Lord Jesus who presents them in His own Name to the Father. What profound importance that understanding gives to praying 'in Jesus' Name'! The Lord Jesus prays all the prayers of His people as they pray in the Spirit in His Name. As the hymn—*Prayer is the soul's sincere desire*—puts it,

No prayer is made on earth alone;
the Holy Spirit pleads;
and Jesus on the eternal throne,
for sinners intercedes.
(James Montgomery)

Prayer in the name of Jesus is a great benefit of the Ascension (John 14:13,14).

We do not have to opt for which of these suggested interpretations are right, because they are all correct. They declare what other Scriptures confirm—always an assurance that we are on solid ground. But we will be least likely to be led into unhelpful by-paths if we concentrate on the interpretation that translates the verb 'to intercede' as 'to look after someone's interests'.

Our Advocate

Associated with the intercession of our Lord Jesus is His position as our Advocate with the Father. John writes, 'My little children, these things I write to you, that you may not sin. And if anyone sins, we have an Advocate with the Father, Jesus Christ the righteous. And He Himself is the propitiation for our sins, and not for ours only but also for the whole world' (1 John 2:1,2). My conviction, which I hope I can now justify, is that this has special reference to the evil work of Satan, the great accuser. The term 'Advocate' implies an accuser or adversary. We have such in the devil, called, in the Book of Revelation, 'the accuser of our brethren, who accused them before our God day and night' (Revelation 12:10). Jewish rabbis spoke of Israel having both an Accuser and a Defender in the court of heaven (cf. Daniel 12:1; Revelation 12:7ff).

Viewed as the sinners we are in God's court, and summoned to appear before His justice, the Lord Jesus is our Advocate, who speaks in our defence, and meets the charges against us. Paul's dramatic words in Romans 8 similarly suggest an accuser or condemner. 'Who is he who condemns?' Paul asks. He answers, 'It is Christ who died, and furthermore is also risen, who is even at the right hand of God, who also makes intercession for us' (Romans 8:34).

The background seems clear: accepted as we are by the Father, at His own initiative, through the work of His Son, we nevertheless still sin, and, sadly, often dishonour Him. The office of our Lord Jesus as Advocate has particular reference therefore to our sins *after our conversion*, for which Satan accuses us in the court of heaven. He has the audacity to appeal to God's justice that we ought to be punished. In our absence, our glorious Advocate takes up our cause. He takes our part before the Father as the Judge of all the earth, and argues against Satan on the ground of His atoning work at Calvary. He does not deny our crimes, but He argues His substitution. He does not deny God's justice, but claims it for us because the price has been paid for our sins. He neither ignores our guilt nor neglects God's law, but through His unique satisfying of God's justice against our sin by His atoning death, and through the power of His advocacy—*and here again it does not need to be vocal*, for His presence as our Saviour at God's right hand declares all that needs to be said—our opponent is thwarted, and

God the Father's justice and mercy are honoured.

The Book of Job provides a telling illustration of Satan's activity as the accuser. 'Now there was a day when the sons of God came to present themselves before the LORD, and Satan also came among them. And the Lord said to Satan, "From where do you come?" So Satan answered the LORD and said, "From going to and fro on the earth, and from walking back and forth on it." Then the LORD said to Satan, "Have you considered My servant Job, that there is none like him on the earth, a blameless and upright man, one who fears God and shuns evil?" So Satan answered the LORD and said, "Does Job fear God for nothing? Have You not made a hedge around him, around his household, and around all that he has on every side? You have blessed the work of his hands, and his possessions have increased in the land. But now, stretch out Your hand and touch all that he has, and he will surely curse You to Your face!" So the LORD said to Satan, "Behold, all that he has is in your power; only do not lay a hand on his person. Then Satan went out from the presence of the LORD' (Job 1:6-12).

Satan no doubt similarly accuses us before God as he witnesses our sins and failures, prompted often by his deliberate provocation and temptations. We require an Advocate who will answer Satan's accusations, and our Lord Jesus is such. As our Substitute, the Lord Jesus has taken our sins as His own. Having acknowledged them to be His, the quarrel is no longer between us and Satan. The Lord Jesus has made it His quarrel. Our Saviour puts our enemy in his place!

When our adversary accuses us before God, our great High Priest, the Man in glory, says in effect to the Father by His established place at the Father's right hand, 'It is true that they are sinners, who deserve wrath and condemnation, but see the wounds in My hands, My feet, My side; these I endured for them; by these I expiated their guilt. Yes, I gave My own life for them. I have satisfied the demands both of law and justice on their behalf. Therefore I look not to Your mercy alone, but to Your justice and faithfulness to forgive them, out of regard for Me, so that You may be just and the justifier of all who believe in Me.' This ties in with John's foundational statement about forgiveness: 'If we confess our sins, He is faithful and just to forgive us our sins and to cleanse us from all unrighteousness' (1 John 1:9). As Job put it, 'Even now my witness is in heaven; and my evidence is on high. ... I know that my Redeemer lives' (Job 16:19; 19:25). If Job had such confidence those centuries before our Saviour's coming, how much more may we possess it in the light of His Cross, Resurrection and Ascension.

The New Testament book that says most about our Lord Jesus Christ's continuing priesthood—the Letter to the Hebrews—urges us, more than any other book, to fix our eyes upon Him (Hebrews 3:1; 12:2). With the eye of faith we are to see our Lord Jesus, our great High Priest, Intercessor and Advocate, at God's right hand. His finished work assures us of our access to God, and our complete security and safety no matter what the enemy of souls may say either to God or our consciences. We may argue as Paul does 'What then shall we say to these things? If God is for us, who can be against us' (Romans 8:31)?

The Giver of the Spirit

The Ascension and the gift of God the Holy Spirit are inseparable. Our Saviour's exaltation opened the way for His presence, by the Spirit, to be with the Church throughout the world, in every generation. Basic to our understanding of this benefit is the revelation the Bible gives that God is a Trinity of Father, Son and Holy Spirit. God the Father gave His Son to be the Saviour we need. The Son achieved salvation by His atoning death upon the Cross. As a fruit of that saving work, God the Father put it within the gift of His Son to bestow the Holy Spirit upon the Church. Believers now possess many benefits believers in the Old Testament did not know.

While active in the Old Testament period, the Holy Spirit was not given in His fullness to all of God's people. Instead, God endued individuals with the Spirit's power for the achievement of immediate and specific tasks. So we read that the Spirit came upon men and women for a period to enable them to accomplish what God especially commissioned them to do (Numbers 11:25; Judges 11:29; 15:14; 1 Samuel 16:13; 1 Chronicles 12:18; 2 Chronicles 24:20; Ezekiel 2:2; 3:24). We read too of the Holy Spirit being withdrawn from an individual (1 Samuel 16:14), and of David praying that the Holy Spirit might not be taken from him (Psalm 51:11).

Jesus explained to His disciples that the Holy Spirit could not be given them until He returned to heaven. 'Nevertheless I tell you the truth. It is to your advantage that I go away; for if I do not go away, the Helper will not come to you; but if I depart, I will send Him to you' (John 16:7). The gift of the Holy Spirit was a glorious consequence of the victory of the Cross that both the Resurrection and Ascension displayed. It was further evidence that the work of reconciliation was accomplished, and that God the Father had set His approval upon it. In the Garden of Eden, Adam and Eve lost the indwelling of the Spirit by their disobedience, and forfeited that gift for all their descendants. When our Lord Jesus, 'the second Man … from heaven' (1 Corinthians 15:47) came, God the Father did not give Him 'the Spirit by measure' (John 3:34). The Spirit is restored to all whom the Last Adam, our Lord Jesus, reconciles to God.

The glorious gift of the Conqueror

The Spirit is the conquering Saviour's gift to His Church. The Lord Jesus received the Holy Spirit in order to bestow Him upon us. Peter was in no doubt about this proper interpretation of Pentecost, when he declared Jesus' exaltation. 'Therefore being exalted to the right hand of God, and having received from the Father the promise of the Holy Spirit, He poured out this which you now see and hear' (Acts 2:33). As John succinctly puts it, 'And of His fullness we have all received, and grace for grace' (John 1:16). At the beginning of Jesus' ministry, John the Baptist promised that Jesus, the Christ, would baptise with the Spirit (Matthew 3:11; Luke 3:16).

The gift of the Spirit is a glorious gift, for, as we have said, He is the Third Person of the Trinity, and is given to us as 'another Helper'. His description as 'another Helper' is highly significant. All the Lord Jesus was to His disciples by His close and intimate relationship with them, He may be to us now by His Spirit. While our Saviour was with His disciples, He taught them, encouraged them, guided and directed them. We receive these identical benefits from our Saviour by His Spirit. No greater gift than God the Holy Spirit could have been given by the Father and Son. In the Book of Esther the Persian King, Xerxes, is said to have given 'gifts according to the generosity of a king' (Esther 2:18), and the gift of the Spirit expresses the even more amazing liberality of the King of kings.

The generous gift of the Spirit is a direct consequence and fruit of our Saviour's mighty conquest over sin, Satan and hell. As our King and Conqueror of all our enemies, our Lord Jesus ascended to receive the gifts promised Him by the Father for His Church. Quoting Psalm 68:18, Paul writes, 'When He ascended on high, He led captivity captive, and gave gifts to men' (Ephesians 4:8). The picture is of a king or general returning home in triumph after battle. It is a picture to which we shall return later in another context.

Great conquests were—and still are—followed by triumphant marches. This was particularly so in ancient times. Behind the victorious general were his captives, and from his hand came the free and liberal distribution of treasures, the results and benefits of his conquest, to share with his own people.

Our hearts—The Saviour's home

The Lord Jesus identifies the Holy Spirit's living within us as His own presence with us. At no time did He do this more clearly than in the conversations in the upper room immediately before the Crucifixion. 'And I will pray the Father, and He will give you another Helper, that He may abide with you forever, even the Spirit of truth, whom the world cannot receive, because it neither sees Him nor knows Him; but you know Him, for He dwells with you and will be in you. I will not leave you orphans; I will come to you. A little while longer and the world will see Me no more, but you will see Me. Because I live, you will live also. At that day you will know that I am in My Father, and you in Me, and I in you' (John 14:16-20). We are not left as orphans, because through the gift of the Spirit, the Lord Jesus, while in heaven as the Man in glory, is also with us. He comes to us individually and corporately by the Holy Spirit's indwelling of our hearts. By the Spirit He is in us, and shows Himself to us, and with the Father makes His home with us (John 14:21,23). By the Spirit we enjoy fellowship with the Father and the Son (1 John 1:3). The Lord Jesus makes His home in our hearts by faith (Ephesians 3:17).

This rich experience is the direct consequence of our Lord's Ascension. It could come about only through His glorification. Gospel writer John records how on the last and greatest day of the Feast of Tabernacles. 'Jesus stood and cried out, saying, "If anyone thirsts, let him come to Me and drink. He who believes in Me, as the Scripture has said, out of his heart will flow rivers of living water." But this,' comments John, 'He spoke concerning the Spirit, whom those believing in Him would receive, for the Holy Spirit was not yet given, because Jesus was not yet glorified' (John 7:37-39). 'Glorified' is John's short-hand for crucified, risen and ascended.

Our Lord Jesus' words show that the experience we have of the Spirit consequent upon His Ascension is something entirely new and different from anything God's people knew before. We are encouraged to picture a stream of water, constantly flowing, or a fountain perpetually gushing forth its refreshing waters. When Peter spoke of the Spirit being 'poured out' on the Day of Pentecost he likewise pointed to the profusion and generosity of the gift.

An important part of the covenant of redemption

In what we sometimes call the covenant of redemption—a covenant entered into before the creation of the world and the beginning of time (Ephesians 1:4; 2 Timothy 1:9), that anticipated human rebellion and the fall—God the Father promised the Son that, as a result of His atoning death, He would give Him an inheritance among all the tribes, peoples and nations of the world. It is an inheritance of 'redeemed' men and women. But how were such believers to be kept and preserved throughout their life in this world in view of the weakness and vulnerability their fallen human nature makes inevitable? The answer was simple yet profound: by the gift of God the Holy Spirit to live in each of them. As Jonathan Edwards expressed it in the seventeenth century, 'The Spirit was the inheritance that Christ, as God-man, purchased for Himself and His Church, or for Christ mystical; and it was the inheritance that He, as God-man, received of the Father, at His Ascension, for Himself and them' (Jonathan Edwards: *Treatise on Grace*, p. 90).

The Gift above all other spiritual gifts

It is by the Holy Spirit that the Lord Jesus gives other gifts to His Church. Chapters 12-14 of 1 Corinthians, Romans 12 and 1 Peter 4:8-11 are key passages concerning these spiritual gifts. These various gifts are all the work of the same Spirit, and are given to individual Christians as the Spirit alone determines, with the common good of the Lord Jesus Christ's people in view. The danger always exists, both through our spiritual immaturity or innate sinfulness, that we may become preoccupied with the gifts rather than with the Giver. Although the Spirit distributes the gifts, He would always have us see behind their distribution the work of our King. He it is who obtained the Holy Spirit for us, and all His gifts and benefits. The words of Dr. A. B. Simpson, founder of *The Christian and Missionary Alliance*, are relevant here:

Once it was the blessing
Now it is the Lord;
Once it was the feeling,
Now it is His Word;

Once His gifts I wanted,
Now the Giver own;
Once I sought for healing
Now Himself alone

Our Lord Jesus' continuing work as Prophet

It is our rightful practice to speak of our Lord Jesus as our Prophet, Priest and King. While His Ascension and position at the Father's right hand plainly relate to His status as Priest and King, they are also significant for His work as our Prophet.

Jesus is the great Prophet of whom Moses spoke when he promised, 'The LORD your God will raise up for you a Prophet like me from your midst, from your brethren. Him you shall hear. ... I ... will put My words in His mouth, and He shall speak to them all that I command Him. And it shall be that whoever will not hear My words, which He speaks in My name, I will require it of him' (Deuteronomy 18:15,18,19). Peter identified the Lord Jesus as this promised Prophet in his speech at the Temple gate called Beautiful after the healing of the crippled beggar: 'For Moses truly said to the fathers, "The LORD your God will raise up for you a Prophet like me from your brethren. Him you shall hear in all things, whatever He says to you. And it shall come to pass that every soul who will not hear that Prophet shall be utterly destroyed from among the people"' (Acts 3:22,23).

The concept of the Lord Jesus as the Prophet is similar to that of Him as the Word—the One through whom God supremely and finally speaks and makes Himself known. He is the One through whom God has spoken and revealed Himself everlastingly. At Jesus' Transfiguration, the Father's words of approval, 'This is My beloved Son' were followed by the clear instruction to the apostles, 'Hear Him!' (Luke 9:35). Those two words underline Jesus' position as the great Prophet to whom we are always to listen.

Calvin expressed this thought powerfully when he quoted Colossians 2:3 in his *Institutes*, that in Christ 'are hidden all the treasures of wisdom and knowledge'. He commented, 'That is, outside Christ there is nothing worth knowing, and all who by faith perceive what He is like have grasped the whole immensity of heavenly benefits. ... And the prophetic dignity in Christ leads us to know that in the sum of doctrine as He has given it to us all parts of perfect wisdom are contained' (Calvin: *Institutes of the Christian Religion, Book II, Chapter XV, Section 2*). This statement is not intended to draw or suggest any distinction between the actual words of Christ recorded in Scripture and the rest of Scripture. Rather it underlines the authority of the whole of the Scriptures because they are His Word (Romans 10:17; Colossians 3:16), inspired by His Spirit (1 Peter 1:10-12), speaking everywhere of Him (Luke 24:27).

When we call the Lord Jesus our Prophet, we affirm that He is our supreme Teacher, to whom we uniquely look for instruction and direction. The One by whom the Lord Jesus teaches us is God the Holy Spirit, significantly called, as we have seen, 'another Helper' (John 14:16). The Lord Jesus taught the apostles to look forward to a renewal of His teaching after His Death, Resurrection and Ascension. 'These things I have spoken to you in figurative language; but the time is coming when I will no longer speak to you in figurative language, but I will tell you plainly about the Father' (John 16:25).

The Holy Spirit, therefore, is the gift of the Lord Jesus, our Prophet, for through Him He continues to teach us. The Spirit's supreme task is not to speak of Himself but to speak *of* our Lord Jesus Christ and *for* Him. The Spirit's work is always in relation to the work of Christ (John 16:8-15). He takes what is Christ's and reveals it to us (John 16:13,14). He does this always by the Scriptures, the Word He has inspired. *The Westminster Larger Catechism* appropriately declares, 'Christ executes the office of a Prophet, in His revealing to the Church, in all ages, by His Spirit and Word, in divers ways of administration, the whole will of God, in all things concerning their edification and salvation.' In other words, all spiritual enlightenment to understand the Scriptures, and the strength that comes through them, flow from our Lord Jesus. He dispenses them to us by His Spirit's working in our minds and hearts. Every time we are challenged, convicted, encouraged and strengthened by the Scriptures, the Spirit is graciously working on our behalf as the gift of the Lord Jesus, our Prophet.

As our Prophet, the Lord Jesus raises up by His Spirit pastors and teachers to be His instruments and messengers to teach and nurture the churches. When congregations are under the proper control and direction of the Spirit, it is the voice of Jesus that His people hear through them.

Mark's gospel ends with the information that after the Lord Jesus' Ascension, the disciples 'went out and preached everywhere, the Lord working with them and confirming the word through the accompanying signs' (Mark 16:20). Although there is some debate about whether or not these concluding words were part of Mark's original writing, their inclusion points to the Church's understanding of the Lord Jesus' work as a Prophet through His disciples. He worked with them confirming His Word. To hear them speak was to hear Him. With this conviction Paul assured the Christians at Rome, 'I know that when I come to you, I shall come in the fullness of the blessing of the gospel of Christ' (Romans 15:29). Whenever the Ascended Lord's servants speak by His Spirit in His Name, God's people are helped and spiritually enriched.

The first three chapters of the Book of Revelation provide special insight into how the Lord Jesus, through His Spirit, uses pastors and teachers in the exercise of His work as our Prophet. The Book begins with a revelation of the Lord Jesus to the apostle John. That disclosure was given him by the Holy Spirit, for John says, 'I was in the Spirit on the Lord's Day' (Revelation 1:10). He heard behind him a loud voice—that of his Ascended Lord—instructing him to write down a message for seven churches in Asia (1:11).

Three features of this revelation to John stand out regarding our Saviour as our Prophet. First, the message is from the Lord Jesus. He is the source. He is the One who speaks. Therefore, each message begins with a statement from the Lord Jesus about Himself. For example, in the first message—that to the church in Ephesus—He says, 'These things says He who holds the seven stars in His right hand, who walks in the midst of the seven golden lampstands' (Revelation 2:1; cf. 2:8; 2:12; 2:18; 3:1; 3:7; 3:14). Each time the emphasis is that 'These things says' the Ascended Lord. The instruction the churches need is that of their Head and Prophet.

Secondly, however, each message is given in the first place to 'the angel' of a church. (These individuals are also described as 'stars' in Revelation 1:20.) It might be thought that this implies that each church has its guardian angel, but that is nowhere taught, or suggested, elsewhere in the Bible. The word 'angel' can equally well be translated 'messenger', and the most obvious explanation is that the term refers to the principal pastor and teacher of each church. The Lord Jesus speaks of holding 'the seven stars in

His right hand' (Revelation 2:1), an indication that pastors are to be completely subject and obedient to Him in all they say and teach. He is the Light of the world, and they are His stars. They are to spread His light, and always point to Him as the source of their enlightenment and spiritual understanding. They are to recognise their duty to be completely under their Master's control, ready to speak and deliver only the message He gives them. They are pre-eminently 'messengers'.

Thirdly, and most significantly, the Holy Spirit's work is mentioned, and seven times in an identical manner: 'He who has an ear, let him hear what the Spirit says to the churches' (Revelation 2:7, 11, 17, 29; 3:6, 13, 22).

To sum up: the message is that of the Lord Jesus; the messengers are His pastors and teachers, but it is the Spirit, the gift of the Ascended Jesus, who conveys that message to the churches through the messengers He raises up and appoints.

The illustration from the Book of Revelation is a further reminder that the Spirit does not speak about Himself but consistently fulfils His ministry in accord with the unique position of the Lord Jesus as our Prophet. In the Old Testament the revelation the Holy Spirit gave of the Lord Jesus Christ and God's saving purposes in Him was similarly as 'the Spirit of Christ' (1 Peter 1:10-12), a description that points to the Lord Jesus as the Supreme Revealer of God and of His will.

The gift of power

The power the Lord Jesus gives His Church is the power of God the Holy Spirit. He promised, 'Most assuredly, I say to you, he who believes in Me, the works that I do he will do also; and greater works than these he will do, because I go to My Father' (John 14:12). Our Lord's presence with the Father is the clue to the power He gives His Church. The energy by which God the Father raised His Son from the dead, and then to His right hand, is the force at work in us, and available to us, as we live in obedience to God (Ephesians 1:19-21).

The 'greater works' the Lord Jesus referred to in John 14:12 must be interpreted by our understanding of His own ministry. At the heart of His mission was His purpose to seek and to save the lost (Luke 19:10). The Church's work is 'greater' because it reaches out to the whole world. It can be 'greater' as Peter discovered on the Day of Pentecost when thousands were converted. The conversion of men and women of all nations is part of the 'greater' work we can do because of our Ascended Saviour's power. No miracle is greater than the new birth of men and women into God's kingdom and the changed and better lives they live. The only explanation for the way the Church turned the first century world upside down by its message, and grew so rapidly, was God's almighty power at work in and through its members. So it has been ever since.

The ability to be spiritual priests

The calling that was once uniquely Israel's is now the spiritual inheritance of all God's people. To Christian believers—whether Jews or Gentiles—Peter wrote, 'You are a chosen generation, a royal priesthood, a holy nation, His own special people, that you may proclaim the praises of Him who called you out of darkness into His marvellous light' (1 Peter 2:9). The New Testament lists a variety of spiritual sacrifices, such as living our everyday life for God (Romans 12:1), loving Him (Mark 12:33), serving Him (2 Timothy 4:6; Philippians 2:17), worshipping Him, working for the common good, sharing with others (Hebrews 13:15,16), and praying (Revelation 8:3,4). As Martin Luther put it, regarding the spiritual sacrifice of prayer, 'The fact that we are all priests and kings means that each of us Christians may go before God and intercede for the other. If I notice that you have no faith or a weak faith, I can ask God to give you a strong faith' (Timothy George, *The Theology of the Reformers*, p. 96). It is the Holy Spirit who helps us to exercise the different aspects of our spiritual priesthood. Our spiritual sacrifices are more pleasing to God than millions of animal sacrifices offered in the past because we offer them 'by Jesus' (Hebrews 13:15) and out of gratitude for God's mercy in Him (Romans 12:1).

The wonder of our Saviour's presence with us

Our Lord Jesus is the Man in glory, as we have seen in chapter 5. He is physically in heaven. Every time we share in the Lord's Supper we are reminding ourselves of His physical absence. Yet at the same time—seemingly paradoxically—we rejoice in His presence, for He promises, 'For where two or three are gathered together in My name, I am there in the midst of them' (Matthew 18:20). His presence with us is spiritual—it is by His Spirit. To quote Calvin again, 'Christ left us in such a way that His presence might be more useful to us—a presence that had been confined in a humble abode of flesh so long as He sojourned on earth. ... Carried up into heaven, therefore, He withdrew His bodily presence from our sight (Acts 1:9), not to cease to be present with believers still on their earthly pilgrimage, but to rule heaven and earth with a more immediate power. But by His ascension He fulfilled what He had promised: that He would be with us even to the end of the world. As His body was raised up above all the heavens, so His power and energy were diffused and spread beyond all the bounds of heaven and earth' (Calvin: *Institutes of the Christian Religion, Book II*, Chapter 16, 14).

The messages to the seven churches in the Book of Revelation provide the delightful insight that the Ascended Lord Jesus 'walks in the midst of the seven golden lampstands', the churches (Revelation 2:1). He is always present, and nothing escapes His notice. Although physically absent, He is amazingly present by His Spirit. His presence is our strength and joy. It is the secret of our protection and well-being. His resources, available by His Spirit, always more than match whatever may be against us. No matter what troubles the Church may experience, our Head's presence guarantees our security.

All too often we are like the disciples when the storm broke out on the lake (Luke 8:23,24). We feel ourselves swamped and in danger of drowning. However, with our Leader with us, we are secure. He can rebuke the winds of opposition and quieten the raging waters that threaten us. No trouble comes without His permission. He permits nothing that will not eventually bring us, or His kingdom, profit.

Thanksgiving and prayer

The Ascended Lord's continuing gift of His Spirit to the Church is a cause for constant thanksgiving. At the same time, in thanking Him for the Holy Spirit, we should always strive to obey the Spirit, for in obeying Him, we obey our Lord Jesus.

The Collect for the Sunday after Ascension Day in *The Alternative Service Book* helpfully focuses upon the immediate strength—or comfort—the Lord Jesus gives through His Spirit. It also assures us that the Spirit will see to it that at the end we shall be where the Lord Jesus now is. Its words are, 'Eternal God, the King of Glory, You have exalted Your only Son with great triumph to Your kingdom in heaven. Leave us not comfortless, but send Your Holy Spirit to strengthen us and exalt us to the place where Christ is gone before, and where with You and the Holy Spirit He is worshipped and glorified, now and for ever. Amen.'

The Great Shepherd of the sheep

Shepherd was a way our Lord Jesus loved to describe Himself. In His conversations with His disciples, particularly as the Cross drew closer, He dwelt upon that self-description more than any other (Matthew 25:32; 26:31; John 10:2-4, 7, 11, 14-16, 26, 27; 21:16,17). Because of the title's familiarity there is a danger of neglecting it, especially by those of us who live in towns and cities rather than the country. Early Christian art—which had emerged long before the close of the fifth century—gives evidence of truths Christians knew to be important. Noteworthy was the regularity of the appearance of the figure of the Good Shepherd (K. S. Latourette, *A History of the Expansion of Christianity, Vol. 1,* p.258). Our Lord Jesus continues in that relationship with His people and exercises perfectly all the functions of that responsibility towards us.

Alongside our Saviour's title of 'Shepherd' goes the complementary description of His people as sheep. The most familiar of psalms, the twenty-third, portrays God as the proper and true Shepherd of His people. The image of us as sheep conveys the thought not only of our need of care but of our natural perversity (Isaiah 53:6). God is the 'Shepherd of Israel' who, while He dwells 'between the cherubim', leads His people 'like a flock' (Psalm 80:1). Using human instruments like Moses and Aaron as under-shepherds, the Lord, the Chief Shepherd, led His people from Egypt 'like a flock', although His 'footsteps were not known' (Psalm 77:19,20). It is not surprising that this title is given to God's Son in relation to His people.

'Shepherd' was an Old Testament picture of the Messiah. 'He shall stand and feed His flock in the strength of the LORD,' Micah proclaimed, 'in the majesty of the name of the LORD His God. And they shall abide, for now He shall be great to the ends of the earth' (Micah 5:4).

A unique relationship

Jesus' description as 'Shepherd' is seldom separated in the New Testament from the Cross. What makes His relationship special to the members of His flock is that He laid down His life for each one (Galatians 2:20). The amazing truth the Ethiopian eunuch came to grips with on the desert road, as Philip explained Isaiah 53, was that the Shepherd accepted the punishment His wayward sheep deserve. 'He was led as a sheep to the slaughter; and like a lamb silent before its shearer, so He opened not His mouth' (Acts 8:32; Isaiah 53:7). No doubt Philip carefully explained an earlier verse in that chapter: 'All we like sheep have gone astray; we have turned, every one, to his own way; and the LORD has laid on Him the iniquity of us all' (Isaiah 53:6). The Lord Jesus bought His sheep with His own blood (Acts 20:28). By His wounds they have been healed (1 Peter 2:24). In heaven, where things are what they ought to be, the sheep never forget what the Shepherd has done. At the heart of their praise is the Cross, and the Shepherd's purchasing of them by His blood for God (Revelation 5:9,10).

Good, great, chief and royal

Three adjectives in the New Testament—*good, great* and *chief*—describe the Lord Jesus as our Shepherd, and they have continuing, instructive and heart-warming relevance to His flock. When we call Him the *good* Shepherd (John 10:14) we are declaring Him to be all that a Shepherd ought to be to His sheep. When we call Him the *great* Shepherd of the sheep (Hebrews 13:20) we are drawing attention to His uniqueness. He is not simply *a* Shepherd but *the* Shepherd. He surpasses to perfection all previous and subsequent examples of pastoral care. Moses was a remarkable spiritual shepherd of God's people (Isaiah 63:11), but the Lord Jesus is greater. He is the *chief* Shepherd because He appoints human shepherds to care for His flock, but they always remain *under*-shepherds, something they and we must never forget.

To these three New Testament adjectives we may add the word *royal*. The Old Testament frequently describes kings and rulers as shepherds, as did many peoples in the ancient near east (Isaiah 44:28; Jeremiah 23:1-6; Micah 5:4,5). The description is given to Moses and David (Isaiah 63:11; Psalm 78:70f). Significantly, they both received their call to leadership while working as shepherds. When God called Joshua to be the leader of God's people, he was also to be their shepherd (Numbers 27:15-21). Our Shepherd, Jesus Christ, is also our King—a title we shall explore later. Far from being a King who lords it over His people, He is a King who cares responsibly and lovingly for each member of His flock.

Knowledge leading to care

A distinctive feature of our Lord Jesus Christ's shepherd care is His personal knowledge of His sheep (John 10:14). The pattern of this knowledge is that which the Father and the Son have of one another (John 10:15). This profound truth—more than any other—emerges in what the Lord Jesus says to His people in the early chapters of the Book of Revelation (1-3). Each of the messages to the churches begins with Jesus' words '*I know*'. To the church at Ephesus, He says, '*I know* your works' (Revelation 2:2). To the church at Smyrna, He says, '*I know* … your tribulation, and poverty' (Revelation 2:9). To the church in Pergamum, '*I know* … where you dwell' (Revelation 2:13). To the church in Thyatira, '*I know* your works, love, service, faith, and your patience; and as for your works, the last are more than the first' (Revelation 2:19). To the church in Sardis, He says, '*I know* your works, that you have a name that you are alive, but you are dead' (Revelation 3:1). To the church in Philadelphia, He says, '*I know* your works' (Revelation 3:8). Finally, to the church at Laodicea, He says, '*I know* your works, that you are neither cold nor hot' (Revelation 3:15). The list is both comprehensive and impressive. He knows our deeds, hard work, perseverance, afflictions, poverty or wealth, circumstances, spiritual battles, love and faith, our reputations (whether true or false), and our spiritual warmth, coldness or lukewarmness.

The Lord Jesus wanted all churches to know that He is the One 'who searches the minds and hearts' (Revelation 2:23). He knew every individual member of each church fellowship—whether Antipas, a faithful witness to Him in Pergamum, or Jezebel, who misled believers in Thyatira (Revelation 2:13,20). The Lord Jesus knows His sheep (John 10:14). We cannot be in any difficulty that He does not see. His knowledge always leads to appropriate action for our safety and well-being, as we shall now see.

Care leading to action

Peter reminds us that we 'have now returned to the Shepherd and Overseer' of our souls (1 Peter 2:25). The addition of the word *Overseer* indicates the action the Shepherd's care dictates when His sheep are in any kind of danger. Douglas MacMillan, a minister of the Free Church of Scotland, was a shepherd before his training for the ministry. In some published talks entitled *The Lord our Shepherd* he gave a lovely illustration of a shepherd's care. 'On our land,' he wrote, 'there was one particular mountain of about 1,500 feet, and from the top of that mountain I could see "every thistle", as we would say—every area where sheep were kept. I used to go up there with a pair of powerful glasses so that I could survey the whole area. I remember being up there once on an early summer morning, when the lambs were getting big. We were troubled by hill foxes (in 1953, for example, we lost 300 lambs because of foxes), so I was out there at half-past three in the morning with binoculars, a .303 rifle and a shepherd's crook. I saw something then that I had never seen before and have never forgotten since. Sitting on top of the hill I could see a fox, way down below me in a flat valley, working sheep just the way a dog works. ... You know how the dogs "wear" the sheep, as we say, gathering them up, bunching them together, driving them, and doing all these wonderful things. Well, here was a fox doing the very same thing way down there below me. All the mothers were in a great state of trial trying to protect their lambs. The fox was actually trying to drive the sheep to a boggy place. He was wanting to get the lambs stuck down, as they were getting big. I waited, because this fox was working better than any collie I had ever seen. I waited a long time, and the sheep were all distressed and troubled. For them the world was turning upside down, and they had eyes only for the fox. Then, when the time came and I could see the fox really going in for the kill, I did something very, very simple. I put two fingers in my mouth and I whistled. The fox was off like a shot.' Douglas MacMillan then commented, 'Now, you see, the shepherd's eyes were on the sheep all the time. He knew precisely what was happening and he had the ability in a moment to shield them from all danger and harm. How much more our Shepherd! He never slumbers; He never sleeps. His eye is on you ...' (J. Douglas MacMillan: *The Lord our Shepherd*, p. 34f. Evangelical Press of Wales).

An incident in the gospels at the time of Jesus' betrayal provides a delightful and encouraging example of our Shepherd's intervention on behalf of His sheep. John writes, 'And Judas, who betrayed Him, also knew the place; for Jesus often met there with His disciples. Then Judas, having received a detachment of troops, and officers from the chief priests and Pharisees, came there with lanterns, torches, and weapons.' Notice now what the Lord Jesus did. 'Jesus therefore, knowing all things that would come upon Him, went forward and said to them, "Whom are you seeking?" They answered Him, "Jesus of Nazareth." Jesus said to them, "I am He." And Judas, who betrayed Him, also stood with them.' Why did Jesus ask this question? Clearly His intention was to remind those who had come to arrest Him that it was He they wanted and not the disciples. 'Then—when He said to them, "I am He,"—they drew back and fell to the ground. Then He asked them again, "Whom are you seeking?" And they said, "Jesus of Nazareth." Jesus answered, "I have told you that I am He. Therefore, if you seek Me, *let these go their way.*"' Jesus deliberately stood between His disciples and those who came to arrest both Him and them. He twice led the soldiers to declare that it was He, and not the disciples, they were seeking. John, the writer of this gospel, recognises Jesus' purpose, and adds, 'That the saying might be fulfilled which He spoke, "Of those whom You gave Me I have lost none"' (John 18:2-9). The Shepherd put Himself between His sheep and their enemies—and this He does still.

Spiritual pasture and undershepherds

Peter's description of the Lord Jesus as the Shepherd and Overseer of our souls properly reminds us that our Shepherd's main concern is our spiritual well-being. Our natural preoccupation is with physical welfare. The more we know our Shepherd and share His concerns, the greater priority we give to our soul. The soul is the seat and centre of our inner life and that immediate or first part of us that receives God's salvation (cf. Philippians 3:20,21). No part of us is more valuable. Charles Wesley aptly wrote a hymn beginning 'Jesus, Lover of my soul'.

For the well-being of our souls, our Shepherd provides the rich and nourishing 'pastures' of His Word, the Scriptures. In David's Shepherd psalm, he declared of God, 'He makes me to lie down in green pastures' (Psalm 23:2). Our souls require the nourishment of the sound teaching of the Bible that rebukes, corrects and trains us in righteousness, so that we 'may be complete, thoroughly equipped for every good work' (2 Timothy 3:16,17).

The apostle Peter never forgot his last personal conversation with his Risen Lord when on three occasions He asked Peter, 'Do you love Me?' Each time that Peter responded by reaffirming his love for his Lord, Jesus instructed him to feed His lambs and sheep and to take care of them (John 21:15-17), and at whatever cost to himself as he followed his Lord's example (John 21:19,22). It is no surprise that when Peter wrote his first letter, he particularly instructed spiritual undershepherds to feed and nurture God's flock under their care (1 Peter 5:2).

Pastors and teachers are the Ascended Shepherd's provision for His Church (Ephesians 4:11). The words 'pastors and teachers' refer to one office. Every pastor must have the ability and desire to teach. No one can genuinely teach God's people without having a pastoral—a shepherd's—heart for them. Some pastors may have more of a teaching gift than others; but all pastors must have some aptitude to teach.

The Lord Jesus' gift of pastors and teachers has our spiritual maturity as its specific end. Ephesians 4:13 describes it as our attaining 'to the measure of the stature of the fullness of Christ.' Our Shepherd purposes the spiritual growth of His flock. He intends us to go from spiritual childhood to spiritual adulthood—from being lambs to mature sheep. There are three steps to this spiritual maturity. First, we are to find our rightful place in the flock so that we make our individual contribution to its well-being by useful works of service. At the same time we are to receive the benefits of the exercise of the spiritual gifts of other members of the flock. We all have a part to play in the spiritual life, health and service of our Saviour's people. Second, we are to reach 'the unity of the faith' (Ephesians 4:13). Spiritual undershepherds' teaching, properly given and received, results in our possessing a growing understanding of 'the faith', and a greater grasp of our hope—and doing so together. Third, we are to attain to 'the knowledge of the Son of God' (Ephesians 4:13). Faith and spiritual growth are not simply a matter of believing facts. Rather, we are to know a Person, our Lord Jesus Christ Himself. A distinctive mark of His sheep is that they know Him and recognise His voice (John 10:3,4). The more we know Him, the more spiritually mature, or full-grown, we become.

The Chief Shepherd's concern reflected in His flock

'Other sheep'—those not yet called into His flock—are our Saviour's equal concern. His purpose is not to mollycoddle those inside the fold, but to reach those outside. 'And other sheep I have which are not of this fold; them also I must bring' the Lord Jesus reminded His disciples. 'And they will hear My voice; and there will be one flock and one shepherd' (John 10:16).

Each sheep is added individually to the flock by the Chief Shepherd, and there is but one fold. We are not saved in isolation from others, but in company with them. Just as the Chief Shepherd directed and guided others to seek us out and bring us to Him, so we must reach out to those who are still lost and distant from Him. We must seek them with the urgency, diligence and self-sacrificing spirit of the Chief Shepherd (Luke 15:4). It is sadly possible to look upon a crowd of people and to be blind to, and oblivious of, their desperate need. Those close to the Shepherd see them as He saw—and sees—them as 'weary and scattered, like sheep having no shepherd' (Matthew 9:36). Obedient members of His flock live in the light of the last judgment when men and women's relationship to the Shepherd will be revealed. 'All the nations will be gathered before Him, and He will separate them one from another, as a shepherd divides his sheep from the goats' (Matthew 25:32).

To have the shout of our King among us, we need to keep close to the Shepherd, always remembering our own proneness as sheep to wander. Close to Him, He will reach out through us to those who are now lost as once we were. When the King's shout is among us, we have eyes to see the vast harvest to be reaped (John 4:35-38), and we determine, 'It shall be done!'

His people's Captain

I feel like a discoverer of an overlooked treasure that deserves to be shared with all who will appreciate its value. This is certainly so with the description of our Lord Jesus Christ's relationship to His people as 'Captain'. Contemporary usage of the word does not help us here. We use it to describe an officer in command of a ship or aircraft, a commissioned officer in the army, the leader of a team sport, or someone in the forefront of a sphere of activity such as 'a captain in industry'. 'Captain' in the Bible—sometimes translated 'prince', 'pioneer' or 'author'—has greater significance. It is a title worth taking afresh into our vocabulary and thinking.

The Old Testament

'Captain' appears among the titles given to the Messiah in Old Testament prophecies. Literally it means 'one lifted up', an apt description of our Saviour's position as the One whose Name is greater than any other, and who is exalted at God the Father's right hand. The prophet Ezekiel uses the title most, and, out of thirty-six occurrences, twenty refer to the Messiah (e.g. Ezekiel 34:24).

Prince, Pioneer, Author and Captain in the New Testament

The title (*archegos*) appears on four occasions in the New Testament. The New King James Version and The New International Version translate it as 'Prince' in Acts 5:31, and the NKJ does the same in Acts 3:15. In Hebrews 2:10 and 12:2 they both translate it as 'Author'. Neither 'prince' nor 'author' in the English language fully convey its significance. When we think of a prince, we probably have in view a member of a royal family, or an inherited title that may mean little. When we have in mind an author, we picture literary activity. It may be because of these rather weak ideas that the word has not established its importance in contemporary Christian thinking, especially in relation to the Lord Jesus' Ascension and His continuing work for us.

Regaining its significance

A captain, prince or author *(archegos)*—is *someone who begins something so others may follow or enter.* We shall need to remind ourselves of this definition as we go on. In ordinary use of the Greek word, the captain or author could describe someone who began a family into which others were born. Abraham, for example, could have appropriately borne the title because of his unique place as the father of the Jewish race, and the spiritual father of all believers.

The 'author' or 'pioneer' could also be a person who established a town in which people then came to live. The idea is essentially of someone who blazes a trail for others to follow. Someone has put it like this, 'Suppose a ship was on the rocks, and suppose the only way to rescue was for someone to swim ashore with a line, so, once the line was secure, others might follow. The one who was first to swim ashore would be the author *(archegos)* of the safety of the others.' The context therefore determines whether we should translate the word as political or military leader, ruler, prince, chief, founder, originator, pioneer, author or captain. The various translations convey the richness of a title we have very much lost, and from the recovery of which we may only benefit. However used, it is always a title of great honour, which explains why it is given to our Lord Jesus Christ.

When Peter gave his defence of his gospel preaching before the Sanhedrin, he explained, 'The God of our fathers raised up Jesus whom you murdered by hanging on a tree. Him God has exalted to His right hand to be *Prince* and Saviour, to give repentance to Israel and forgiveness of sins' (Acts 5:30,31). Exaltation to God's right hand is shown here to be synonymous with our Lord Jesus' position as Prince *(archegos)*—He is highly lifted up. His authority as the Saviour is such that He alone may bestow the gift of repentance and forgiveness of sins (Acts 5:31). As we receive that gift, we then delight to honour His Name and confess it before the world. We rejoice to have Him as our Benefactor for our affairs are His personal concern. In Him we have the best of princes, and the finest of lords.

The manner in which we think of our Ascended Lord and understand His relationship to us determines the way in which we live. For that reason it is vital that we possess the New Testament understanding of this title in three ways.

The Author of life

First, our Lord Jesus Christ is *the Author of life* to His people. As mortal men and women in a dying world, we cannot exaggerate the significance of this. Peter employed this description when he spoke to amazed onlookers at the remarkable healing of the crippled beggar at the Temple gate called Beautiful. 'You,' he declared, 'killed the *Prince of life*, whom God raised from the dead' (Acts 3:15).

Jesus Christ, the Son of God, is the source of *all* life (John 1:4). It is because there is life in Him that there is life anywhere in the world. Many forms of life exist. We all possess biological life. We live and breathe the world's atmosphere, and enjoy the benefits of physical existence. However, there is another kind of life—spiritual or eternal life. C. S. Lewis regarded the difference as so important that he gave them two distinct names. 'The biological sort which comes to us through Nature, and which (like everything else in Nature) is always tending to run down and decay so that it can only be kept up by incessant subsidies from Nature in the form of air, water, food, etc., is *Bios*. The spiritual life which is in God from all eternity, and which makes the whole natural universe, is *Zoe*. *Bios* has, to be sure, a certain shadowy or symbolic resemblance to *Zoe*: but only the sort of resemblance there is between a photo and a place, or a statue and a man. A man who changed from having *Bios* to having *Zoe* would have gone through as big a change as a statue which changed from being a carved stone to being a real man. And that is precisely what Christianity is about. This world is a great sculptor's shop. We are the statues and there is a rumour going round the shop that some of us are one day going to come to life' (*Mere Christianity*, Book IV, chapter 1). We forfeited this *Zoe* through the disobedience of our first parents, Adam and Eve, a disobedience we ourselves have repeated. Through our Lord Jesus Christ it may be recovered.

The amazing truth of the Incarnation is that for our sakes Jesus became a man, took upon Himself our humanity (apart from sin) and allowed Himself to be put to death, the penalty of our sin, as our Sin-bearer. He truly died. But when He died, death also died for, on the third day He rose again! He rose to be the source—*the Author (archegos)*—of eternal life to all who believe in Him. He came that we might have life, *Zoe*, better than we ever thought possible (John 10:10).

The teaching of the New Testament is that whoever believes in God's only begotten Son has eternal life (John 3:36). Sin's power to separate our souls from God was shown to be over when He rose again. Its iron grip is broken for all who believe in Him. His Resurrection assures us of God's forgiveness: He 'was raised because of our justification' (Romans 4:25). No longer can sin separate us from God. As our *Captain*, He made possible a new beginning that we might follow after and enter into all its benefits.

There is yet more! Our Lord Jesus Christ rose again as 'the firstfruits of those who have fallen asleep' (1 Corinthians 15:20). He began something here too that we might follow after Him. His Resurrection is the prototype of ours as believers. He was the first to be raised from the dead to die no more. He was the first to be raised and to be glorified in His humanity. In His Resurrection we have the pledge that we will share our Captain's destiny. He is *the Author of Resurrection life* for us.

This assurance of resurrection is to be often in our thoughts and upon our lips. We are resurrection people, 'sons of the resurrection' (Luke 20:36). Our Lord's Resurrection particularly assures us of God's almighty power. No problem we ever face can be as hopeless as the cold tomb, in which our Saviour's dead body was placed, must have appeared to the first disciples. But God raised Him, and exalted Him to be our Captain—*the Author of life*. By the gift of His Holy Spirit, His Resurrection power is now ours. His Resurrection gives the promise of God's ultimate triumph over death and all its consequences. Often we and our families and friends face human tragedy and bereavement, but our Captain assures us that they will all be put right at the resurrection. No wonder Paul says to Timothy, his young associate, 'Remember that Jesus Christ, of the seed of David, was raised from the dead according to my gospel' (2 Timothy 2:8). When the shout of our King is among His people, they live as resurrection people and never more so than when they experience bereavement. They grieve, but not as those without hope, but instead as those with everything to look forward to in the future (1 Thessalonians 4:13).

Author of salvation

Secondly, our Lord Jesus is *the Author* or *Pioneer of salvation* to His people (Hebrews 2:10). In considering the Lord Jesus as such, it is helpful to keep before us the definition of the *archegos* as *someone who begins something so others may enter into it*. By His death as our Substitute, and then His rising again, He has become the *Author* (the *Prince* or *Captain*) of *our Salvation* (Acts 5:31). He obtained salvation for us, and no one else could have achieved it. As its source, He grants us the gift of repentance and forgiveness of sins (Acts 5:31). We do not always think of repentance as a gift, but without His Spirit working in our hearts we would never seek salvation of our own accord. He then bestows upon us the gift of the forgiveness of our sins—a glorious and perfect fruit of His death.

Crucial to living the Christian life is our remembering the One who achieved our salvation. Experience shows we can lose sight of the centrality of our Lord Jesus in the plan of salvation. Our human nature is so sinful and deceitful that, having believed on Him for salvation, we may fall into the error of relying upon our works—our 'good' works as believers—rather than on the Lord Jesus alone. Even as Jews foolishly transferred their faith from God to circumcision, so we may transfer our faith from our Saviour to outward acts that symbolise our faith, such as baptism and church membership.

One purpose of the regular meeting of God's people around the Lord's Table is to underline how Jesus' death is at the heart of our salvation and our relationship with God. It is spiritually healthy to long that we may never boast except in the Cross of our Lord Jesus Christ (Galatians 6:14). While we are to be Resurrection people, primarily we are to be people of the Cross. Unashamed of the Cross, we are to keep our Saviour's atoning work at the centre of our living and preaching. When the shout of our King is among us as His people, His Cross is our theme.

An important benefit of this description of the Lord Jesus as *the Captain of our salvation* is that it reminds us that our experience of His saving power is present and future, and not only past. Salvation is not our Lord's occasional act, but His continuous activity on behalf of His people. We rightly look back and marvel at His grace in first bringing us into an experience of salvation, especially the forgiveness of our sins, and the transforming work of His Spirit as He changes the direction of our lives. Our need of His delivering power, however, remains: not a day passes without our having to engage in a battle against temptation. Temptations take a variety of forms at different stages of life, but their basic reality and force do not change. As we deliberately look to our Captain, who personally knew the full force of temptation without giving into it, we may obtain both strength and courage to overcome. A hymn expresses it well:

In your hearts enthrone Him;
There let Him subdue
All that is not holy,
All that is not true;
Crown Him as your Captain
In temptation's hour;
Let His will enfold you
In its light and power.
(Caroline Maria Noel)

The Captain of our salvation is 'able to save to the uttermost those who come to God through Him, since He ever lives to make intercession for them' (Hebrews 7:25). Our testimony as His people is not that we live beyond the reach of temptation, but that our Captain daily delivers us as we look to Him. Our testimony is not that we are already perfect, but that our Captain's support is.

Besides personal experience of Jesus' delivering power, we need it corporately in our local congregations. Crises and situations occur in churches that threaten God's honour and the advance of His Son's kingdom. Issues arise that endanger the unity of the church, and sometimes with disastrous consequences. Our first resort should be to look to our Captain, and to ask for His deliverance. The early Church's progress was under constant threat but it was never stronger than when its members unitedly sought their Captain's honour and prayed together in His Name (e.g. Acts 4:23-31; 12:1-19). When the King's shout is among His people, deliverance is what we ask for, expect and experience.

The necessary element of suffering

We must not pass over this title of Jesus as *'the Author of salvation'* too quickly. In the context of our Captain's leadership of His people to glory, the writer to the Hebrews reminds us that it was fitting that God should make the *Author* of our salvation 'perfect through sufferings' (Hebrews 2:10). For Jesus in His Incarnation, suffering came before glory. The same may be true for us—and, to some extent at least, must be. Unmistakably, the Lord Jesus taught His disciples that this was a pattern they could not hope to avoid, and that they should be prepared to expect (i.e. John 16:33).

Although it cannot be described as a primary emphasis, our Lord clearly teaches us to anticipate and to accept suffering and difficulty as we follow Him to glory. Our union with Him—essential to the experience of salvation—means that in some measure at least our Saviour's sufferings are to be shared by us. As we live out our lives in the world, following Him with 'glory' in view, the path we are called to follow may lead to a variety of hard times and bitter experiences. The Bible intimates that the road by which God brings His sons and daughters to glory is full of difficulties, perplexities and oppositions from Satan. The first missionaries of the early Church witnessed to new believers that 'we must through many tribulations enter the kingdom of God' (Acts 14:22).

For some, the suffering may be physically terrifying, as it was for Stephen and all who have suffered martyrdom—and who will yet undergo it—on account of their loyalty to their Master. It may be the suffering that results from obedience to the call of the Lord Jesus to take the gospel to those who have never heard it. That may require going to countries distant from our own, a call that cuts across the natural requirements and preferences of family and human comfort. The demands of Christian service, sometimes, like the care of the churches, may weigh heavily upon us, spoiling our sleep, and affecting our health (2 Corinthians 11:28). To serve the body of Christ faithfully may involve a diversity of sufferings (Colossians 1:24). It is not that we should go around looking for them, or even find pleasure in them. Yet we must accept the principle, and not shirk the Cross in our life.

We may even be privileged to fill up in our flesh what is still lacking regarding our Lord Jesus Christ's afflictions, for the sake of His body, which is His Church (Colossians 1:24). Our Captain's saving work alone could accomplish the Church's salvation, but the gathering in of His people, and their shepherding, require the unreserved and costly service of His people. Only His sufferings could provide propitiation for sin. But effective propagation of the good news of those sufferings often demands suffering on the part of His Church.

The sufferings of the Lord Jesus may overflow into our lives (2 Corinthians 1:5). Such a prospect need not cause us to be anxious or make us flinch. Our *Captain* (*archegos*) will guide and carry us through. By His Spirit and the Scriptures—and not least by the assurance of the victory He has won—He provides every necessary encouragement.

The Lord Jesus has provided an example of what it means to obey God's will, to accept suffering as God's will, and then to enter into glory. It is an axiomatic principle of the Christian life that 'it has been granted' to us 'on behalf of Christ, not only to believe in Him, but also to suffer for His sake' (Philippians 1:29). Since God the Father saw fit to make the Captain or Pioneer of our salvation 'perfect through sufferings' (Hebrews 2:10), it makes complete sense that God should choose to accomplish His purposes in and through us in a similar way. Our heavenly Father has predestined us to be conformed to the likeness of His Son (Romans 8:29). This conformity must be not only in holiness and glory, but also in a degree of suffering.

To acknowledge Jesus as our Captain is to rejoice to be counted worthy to suffer for His sake (Acts 5:41). It means accepting the principle that if we would reign with Him, we must be prepared to suffer for Him (2 Timothy 2:12). A servant cannot expect to be above his master, or a soldier above his captain. Our Lord calls us to take up our cross daily and to follow Him (Luke 9:23). When the shout of our King is among His people, we want 'to fight and not to heed the wounds' so long as we have the reward of doing our Captain's will. When 'the shout of a King' is among us, we do not complain about the difficulties of discipleship or the cost of following in His footsteps. Instead, we rejoice in the privilege!

The Author of our faith

Thirdly, the Lord Jesus is *the Author of our faith*. Every believer possesses a unique ability to look to Jesus. It is a spiritual gift that means nothing to those who do not believe, and that they may even consider to be a nonsense.

The explanation of this faculty is the gift to all believers of God the Holy Spirit, who enables us with the eye of faith to see what the physical eye cannot. Believers may copy Moses who 'endured as seeing Him who is invisible' (Hebrews 11:27). So the writer to the Hebrews urges us to turn our eyes to the Ascended Lord Jesus, 'the *author (archegos)* and finisher of our faith, who for the joy that was set before Him endured the cross, despising the shame, and has sat down at the right hand of the throne of God' (Hebrews 12:2). Again, we need to keep in mind the definition of a captain as one who begins something so others might follow and enter into it.

The Lord Jesus is the *Author* or *Captain* of our faith because He is its source. By His work for us, He laid the foundations of our faith (Hebrews 1:3). It is not for nothing that we sing,

My hope is built on nothing less
than Jesus' blood and righteousness.
(Edward Mote)

He is responsible for our faith's birth, nurture and continuance. He is the object of our faith. Through Him we believe in God (1 Peter 1:21). His Spirit caused faith to come to birth when His Word was sown in our hearts. Although we may know nothing of the details of each other's coming to faith, what happened was straightforward. In different ways we were brought to see the complete trustworthiness of Jesus Christ as the Son of God, the Saviour, who died for sinners, and who invites us to come to Him for salvation. We did exactly that, and in so doing we put our trust in Him, and received a right relationship with God—we were justified through faith.

The manner in which our faith began—*looking to Jesus*—is the way it grows. The secret of great faith is not our capacity to believe but our possession of a great Saviour. Great faith has a great opinion of the Lord Jesus. As Andrew Bonar wrote in his diary, 'I see that faith is high just when our thoughts about our Lord Himself are high and great and satisfying' (Andrew Bonar: *Diary and Letters*, p.327). Our confidence is not in faith, but in the One in whom we trust. As good soldiers of Jesus Christ, we are to fix our eyes upon our Captain. Then we shall have confidence for every battle into which He calls us. When the King's shout is among us, faith is high because our eyes are upon our King.

The Lord Jesus is *the Author of our faith* in a further sense. He is the example of faith we are to follow. As perfect man in His Incarnation—the Last Adam (1 Corinthians 15:45)—He has shown us how to live out in an often hostile world a life of faith in God. For a little over thirty years our Lord Jesus lived on earth trusting His Father for everything. He resorted to prayer, as a daily feature of His life. The writer to the Hebrews records that 'in the days of His flesh, when He had offered up prayers and supplications, with vehement cries and tears to Him who was able to save Him from death, and was heard because of His godly fear' (Hebrews 5:7). Knowing He did not live by bread alone, He studied, knew, loved and lived by the Scriptures. Trusting and obeying God—the two terms are almost synonymous—He went to the Cross. 'Who, when He was reviled, did not revile in return; when He suffered, He did not threaten, but committed Himself to Him who judges righteously' (1 Peter 2:23). He kept hold of faith right to the end. His last words before He died were, 'Father, into Your hands I commend My spirit' (Luke 23:46).

Our Lord Jesus, our Captain, has demonstrated what faith in God means in practice: He blazed the trail. He displayed in His own life the obedience and reward of faith. We must not—we dare not—live the Christian life without expecting faith to be tested. I say 'dare not' because if we do not anticipate such tests they may bowl us over and we may forfeit the blessing God intends we should receive through them. Rather, when tests to our faith come, we are to remember our Captain, look to His example, and know that our faith in Him is 'much more precious than gold that perishes, though it is tested by fire' (1 Peter 1:7). From start to finish the Christian life is a life of faith, so much so that without faith it is impossible to please God (Hebrews 11:6). When our eyes are upon our Captain, and His shout is among us, we recognise the privilege it is to trust God and the *good* fight that the fight of faith is (1 Timothy 6:12)!

Recapturing the picture

A benefit of the title 'Captain' is that it puts into proper focus the conflict that is inevitable in the Christian life. A battle has to be fought against the world, the flesh and the devil. The world will frequently suggest that death is the end of everything, and that the best philosophy is to live for fleeting pleasures rather than God's will. Our Captain, the Prince of life, gives the lie to that, and fills us with resurrection hope and confidence. Our flesh—urged on by the devil—tempts us to think that sin cannot be mastered, and that problems and difficulties are sure to overcome us and mar our testimony as God's people. Nevertheless, our Captain promises deliverance, for greater is He that is in us than He that is in the world (1 John 4:4). When our eyes are upon Him, we possess the secret of strength and victory. An unbelieving world may ignore, and even mock and scorn, faith. Yet the faith that our Captain generates 'sees' in the dark, and lives by His unfailing promises.

Our Captain is the Resurrection and the Life, the Source of eternal salvation, and the Author and Inspirer of our faith. He blazed a trail that we may follow. He does not call us to any path of difficulty He has not first trodden before us. His Resurrection is to be ours—He is *the Author of life*. He, *the Captain of our salvation*, gained all the blessings of salvation for us, and God's purpose is that we should enter into them all. We must not try to escape the reality of the Cross in human experience. Following His example, with the eyes of our faith upon its Author and Perfecter, He will see us through.

The Head of the Church

We cannot overstate the dignity and majesty of our Lord Jesus Christ. His Ascension and sitting at the Father's right hand draw attention to the unique position and authority He has both in the Church and in the world. Authority was His as the Second Person of the Trinity before His Incarnation. At His Ascension, however, He spoke of possessing 'All authority … in heaven and on earth' and of it having 'been given' to Him (Matthew 28:18).

Daniel's anticipation of the glorified Messiah provided the same emphasis. He declared, 'Then to Him was given dominion and glory and a kingdom, that all peoples, nations, and languages should serve Him. His dominion is an everlasting dominion, which shall not pass away, and His kingdom the one which shall not be destroyed' (Daniel 7:14). The implication is that it is in His glorified humanity that He has been given this authority, and as our representative. God the Father gave His Son this authority before time began (Psalm 2:8), but His sovereign plan required the Son's fulfilment of His saving work for us, a work accomplished by His Death, Resurrection and Ascension.

When God raised the Lord Jesus from the dead, He 'seated Him at His right hand in the heavenly places, far above all principality and power and might and dominion, and every name that is named, not only in this age but also in that which is to come' (Ephesians 1:20,21). In every sphere of life we find varying grades of command, dignity and responsibility. Paul takes us through successive human descriptions of importance—rule, authority, power, dominion and titles—and declares the Lord Jesus to be above them all. His dignity has no parallel anywhere in the universe.

The apostle John caught glimpses of the majesty and glory of our Lord Jesus' authority, an authority He has received from the Father (Revelation 2:27). He is the Ruler of God's creation (Revelation 3:14) and of the sovereigns of the earth (Revelation 1:5). He holds the key of David: 'He … opens and no one shuts, and shuts and no one opens' (Revelation 3:7). This is a way of expressing that He alone can admit men and women into God's kingdom. He holds the keys of death and Hades (Revelation 1:18). Our eternal destiny is in His hands.

Head of the Church

Nowhere is the Lord Jesus' authority more plain than in regard to His Church—He is her Head. Even as we cannot think sensibly of our own physical body apart from our head, so it is with Jesus and His Church. The two cannot be separated, or properly considered apart. His body, the Church, is the sphere of His present activity in the world. When the body suffers, He suffers (Matthew 25:35ff; Colossians 1:24). When the body preaches, He preaches. When her message is heard, He is heard. He is the source of the Church's vitality and power. Apart from Him, we can do nothing (John 15:5). He chooses to be dependent upon His body for the carrying out of His saving purposes as its members act in obedience to His last commission. The relationship between the Lord Jesus and His people is so close and fundamental that as the body cannot function without its Head, so the Head is incomplete without His Church (Colossians 1:24).

An infinite love

As her Head, the Lord Jesus loves the body, His Church. Whenever the New Testament urges us to understand the feelings of the Lord Jesus for His people it concentrates uniquely upon His love (Ephesians 5:25). What He Himself said to His first disciples is true for us too, 'As the Father loved Me, I also have loved you' (John 15:9).

We cannot properly look at the Cross and ponder its significance without being assured and overwhelmed by the lavish extent of the Lord Jesus' love. His present love for the members of His body is the same love that took Him to the Cross. This is a truth to take into our thinking. John records the last hours Jesus spent with His disciples in the upper room. He prefaces his account with the comment, 'Having loved His own who were in the world, He loved them to the end' (John 13:1). Jesus' washing of the disciples' feet at the Last Supper and His death upon the Cross, simply and powerfully expressed His undying love for those first disciples and all who, like us, have come after them.

The Holy Spirit gave Paul an awareness of the unfathomable dimensions of the Lord Jesus' love for His people. Expressing his prayer for the Ephesians, he wrote, 'I bow my knees to the Father of our Lord Jesus Christ ... that He would grant ... that you, being rooted and grounded in love, may be able to comprehend with all the saints what is the width and length and depth and height—to know the love of Christ which passes knowledge; that you may be filled with all the fullness of God' (Ephesians 3:14, 16-19). Jesus' love has a breadth, length, depth and height that are utterly beyond our power to take in. It is like an unfathomable ocean. It 'passes knowledge' in that we are always in its school, from which we never graduate!

A sure protection

As Head of the Church, the Lord Jesus safeguards the well-being and interests of His body. His position as our Priest, Shepherd, Captain and King further underline this assurance. His message in the Book of Revelation to the first of the seven churches of Asia was to that at Ephesus. He introduced it by describing Himself as the One 'who holds the seven stars in His right hand, who walks in the midst of the seven golden lamp-stands' (Revelation 2:1). The picture signifies that He has the Church, and the local churches that constitute it, firmly in His grasp. He is unceasing in His watchful care of His people.

The Church has always had subtle and powerful enemies. The world's hatred of the Lord Jesus inevitably rubs off on to her members (John 15:18ff). The New Testament letters, and *Acts* in particular, provide ample evidence of the perpetual opposition the Church faces, and the skilful and crafty attacks of Satan, the enemy of God and the body of Christ.

What the enemies of the Church do may be secretly planned and totally invisible to us. Our all-knowing Head, however, sees all they do, and antic-ipates their every move. This explains why the opponents of the Church continually overreach themselves. Many over the years have prophesied the end of the Church, as recent church history in China and the former Soviet Union illustrates. All such predictions have proved false. The same may be confidently anticipated as the outcome of current prophecies of the Church's doom elsewhere. A Roman general Antigonus overheard his soldiers discussing the potentially overwhelming numbers of the opposing force of their enemies. As a consequence they discouraged and demoralised one another. Antigonus stepped forward and stood among them. He asked a simple question, 'How many would you put in exchange for me?' Our Saviour is more than match for all His enemies and ours. Our shout legitimately is, therefore, 'We are more than conquerors through Him who loved us' (Romans 8:37).

When we recognise the weaknesses and frailties of the Church, and the staggering opposition she has confronted throughout two millennia, the only explanation for her preservation is her Head's almighty power. The Church's many failures only underline the Church's dependence, not upon the courage and energy of its members, but on the power and authority of her Head. Essential to our Head's continuing work in heaven is His keeping, helping and perfecting His people. He knows always what we need and how best to provide it.

The secret of the body's unfailing growth

As the Head of the Church, the Lord Jesus adds members to His body. Throughout His three years' ministry men and women were irresistibly drawn to put their faith in Him, and to become His disciples. *What He began to do and teach, He continues to do through His body.* Contemporary believers are evidence of the amazing activity of the Lord Jesus through His people's proclamation of the good news of salvation. Each has a unique testimony to hearing the Head of the Church's voice and responding personally to His grace and power. His power alone is sufficient to bring us to repentance and faith and then to change us from rebels to committed followers. We may persuade people to make a superficial profession of faith but only the Lord Jesus by His Spirit can bring saving faith to birth. Every true believer is a trophy of His grace.

Acts chapter 2 describes the formation and establishment of the early Church following upon the outpouring of God the Holy Spirit at Pentecost. 'That day about three thousand souls were added to them' (Acts 2:41). So it went on with more and more believing in the Lord and being added to their number (Acts 5:14), including large numbers of the Jewish priests (Acts 6:7). *The Acts of the Apostles* concludes with Paul 'with all confidence, no one forbidding him' preaching the kingdom of God and teaching about the Lord Jesus Christ in the capital of the Roman Empire (Acts 28:30,31). He did this less than thirty years after our Saviour's Ascension and instruction to His disciples to take the gospel to all the world.

The growth of the early Church was not the work and achievement of men and women, but of our Saviour. While the growth came by the preaching of the good news of Jesus, after the pattern of the apostolic preaching at Pentecost, the blessing and growth had but one source—the Lord Jesus Himself. It was 'the Lord' who 'added to the church daily those who were being saved' (Acts 2:47). When the title 'Lord' stands on its own in the New Testament, as here, it nearly always refers to God the Son, the Second Person of the Trinity.

The Lord Jesus has the unique prerogative of adding new members to His body. Our duty, as members already of that body, is to welcome them as He has welcomed us (Romans 15:7). The early Christians were in no doubt concerning our Saviour's prerogative, and it was a truth in which they were carefully instructed. The Corinthian Christians, for example, clearly owed much to Paul's evangelistic activity since he was the first to share the gospel with them. Behind that missionary enterprise however was the clear direction of Paul's Master, the Head of the Church. When the going in Corinth became tough, and it would have been easy to have thrown in the towel and moved on, 'the Lord spoke to Paul in the night by a vision, "Do not be afraid, but speak, and do not keep silent; for I am with you, and no one will attack you to hurt you; for I have many people in this city." And he continued there a year and six months, teaching the word of God among them' (Acts 18:9-11). The Director of Operations is the Head of the Church.

Several times in his letters to the Corinthians, Paul reminded them of the principle he stated in 1 Corinthians 3:6: 'I planted, Apollos watered, but God gave the increase.' While he and Apollos had necessary tasks to fulfil, they were 'but ministers' through whom the Corinthians came to believe (1 Corinthians 3:5). Luke, a close associate of Paul, and well acquainted with his emphases, understood Paul's explanation for every addition to the body of Christ. Describing Lydia's conversion—the first person converted in Philippi—he wrote, 'The Lord opened her heart to heed the things spoken by Paul' (Acts 16:14).

As new believers are added to the body, at our Saviour's initiative, they are fitted together perfectly in the whole body. Each member in his or her special way is intended to help the other parts, so that the whole body may be healthy and grow in love and usefulness (Ephesians 4:15,16).

The unseen Presence and secret of power

As the Head of the Church, the Lord Jesus works with His disciples as they obey His commission to proclaim the gospel. Having declared His authority to His apostles and disciples, the Lord Jesus instructed them, 'Go therefore and make disciples of all the nations, baptising them in the name of the Father and of the Son and of the Holy Spirit, teaching them to observe all things that I have commanded you' (Matthew 28:19-20). He then added, 'And lo, I am with you always, even to the end of the age.'

Jesus fulfils this promise to each generation of believers. Mark's gospel ends with the significant comment: 'So then, after the Lord had spoken to them, He was received up into heaven, and sat down at the right hand of God. And they went out and preached everywhere, the Lord working with them and confirming the word through the accompanying signs' (Mark 16:19,20). *The Acts of the Apostles* provides the best commentary on this statement. 'The Lord working with them' (Mark 16:20) is the explanation of all the progress Acts describes. Acts 11 summarises the activities of persecuted and scattered Christians. It puts together two statements, and the first explains the second. It says, 'And the hand of the Lord was with them, and a great number believed and turned to the Lord' (Acts 11:21).

Everywhere and in every age God's people have borne testimony to the Lord Jesus' presence with them as they obeyed His last command. Feeling abandoned by many people as he obeyed his Lord, Paul was able to write, 'But the Lord stood with me and strengthened me, so that the message might be preached through me, and that all the Gentiles might hear. And I was delivered out of the mouth of the lion' (2 Timothy 4:17). Christians are the Lord's fellow-workers (2 Corinthians 6:1), for whom He takes personal responsibility. While the work of building His Church is essentially His as the Head, He gives His body the privilege of sharing in it. As His fellow-workers, we may be sure of His presence with us. Samuel Rutherford was imprisoned for his loyalty to his Saviour. He wrote, 'Jesus Christ came into my cell last night, and every stone glowed like a ruby.' David Livingstone's testimony was that it was not just he who went tramping through the interior of Africa, but David Livingstone and Jesus Christ together. John and Audrey Coleman and Miss Jean Waddell, British missionaries, experienced imprisonment in Iran, and were released in 1981.

When they arrived at London Heathrow airport they were interviewed by newspaper and television reporters. Audrey Coleman summed up their experience: 'I cannot truthfully say that one has enjoyed every minute of these past seven months, but I would like to record my thanks to the Lord Jesus Christ who has been in control of this whole situation and has given us His strength and encouragement and allowed us to know the truth of His promise that He will never leave us, or forsake us.'

As the Almighty Head of the Church, the Lord Jesus gives her power to do great works in His Name. 'Most assuredly, I say to you, he who believes in Me, the works that I do he will do also; and greater works than these he will do, because I go to My Father' (John 14:12). The authority of the Name of the Head of the Church is the secret of the Church's effectiveness in proclamation and service (Acts 3:6,16).

Perfect knowledge and discipline

Immediately anything affects or touches our body a message is sent to our brain. The head—the brain—possesses incredible knowledge of, and sensitivity to, the body. As the Head of the Church, the Lord Jesus likewise knows the needs of His body, and all that goes on among its members. In considering the Lord Jesus as the great Shepherd, we saw the implications of this in His knowledge and feeding of His sheep.

From His knowledge of His body arises also His salutary discipline of her. For example, the Lord Jesus held it against the church at Thyatira that she tolerated the false teaching of the woman named Jezebel. He promised to give her time for repentance. If that was not fruitful, however, punishment was to follow (Revelation 2:20-23). He warned the church at Ephesus that because of the heights from which they had fallen, He would come and remove their lampstand from its place if they did not repent (Revelation 2:5). He told the lukewarm church at Laodicea, 'As many as I love, I rebuke and chasten' (Revelation 3:19).

One reason Christians are to examine themselves whenever they share in the Lord's Supper is to ensure that their relationship both to the Head and to the members of His body is right. Through neglect of this necessary self-examination, many among the first-century Corinthian Christians became weak and sick, and a number of them died (1 Corinthians 11:30).

Paul saw in this the Head of the Church's discipline of His people for their eternal good (1 Corinthians 11:31,32).

No greater tragedy exists than for the body of Christ to lose sight of her vital relationship to her Head. When she lives in the light and joy of that union, His shout is with her.

King and Governor

Besides His position as Head of the Church, the Ascended Lord Jesus is also His people's King and the Governor of the whole universe. The two descriptions are not identical, though they go closely together. Inevitably there is a measure of overlapping about the titles given to our Lord Jesus, but each makes its own distinctive contribution to our understanding.

A Messianic anticipation

As we saw in Chapter Two, at the centre of Old Testament expectation was the confidence that God's King, the Messiah, would bring men and women of every nation into obedience to Himself, ultimately destroying every enemy of God and His people, and judging all, to the ends of the earth. No ordinary human king could achieve such expectation, only the One installed at the Father's appointment (Psalm 2:6). The Ascension was the outworking of these glorious purposes and promises.

A position of authority

At the Ascension, Jesus returned to heaven. Heaven is always viewed in the Bible as the place of authority because it is God's dwelling place. Daniel declares, 'Heaven rules' (Daniel 4:26), another way of saying 'God rules'. Jesus' Ascension was the occasion of His enthronement in the place of supreme authority in the universe (Matthew 28:18; Mark 14:62). His power is unlimited and His honour without parallel. He ascended into heaven that He might be supreme over all the powers of heaven and earth (Colossians 1:16-18). As Paul expressed it in his letter to the Ephesians, 'He who descended is also the One who ascended far above all the heavens, that He might fill all things' (Ephesians 4:10). Whatever else His filling the whole universe includes, it must mean that He is the One who carries through God's purposes for everything God has made. Through Him God's will is done and accomplished for all creation.

His people's King

The Lord Jesus is already King of kings and Lord of lords because that is God's ultimate purpose. However, we do not yet see that worked out and acknowledged in the world, as ultimately it will be. Nevertheless, His people already know the Lord Jesus to be their Lord and King, and they delight to acknowledge Him as such. Nowhere is this clearer than in the Book of Revelation. The main vision of that book is of Jesus as King, a vision all Christians are meant to share. What impressed John above all was the boundless nature of the authority our Lord Jesus Christ has received from the Father (Revelation 2:27).

The Lord Jesus' Kingship was prominent in the teaching of the apostles. The accusation made against Paul and Silas at Thessalonica, though false in its motive and unhelpful in its misconstruction of their words, was true in its assertion about Jesus. Their opponents declared, 'They are all acting contrary to the decrees of Caesar, saying there is another king—Jesus' (Acts 17:7). The early Christians knew that Jesus' sitting at the right hand of the Father draws attention to the unique position the Father has given Him of kingly power and authority over angels, authorities, and powers in heaven and on earth. As the writer to the Hebrews appropriately asks, 'But to which of the angels has He ever said: "Sit at My right hand, till I make Your enemies Your footstool"' (Hebrews 1:13).

A kingship that is different

Our Saviour's present exercise of His Kingship is different, however, from any other. 'My kingdom,' He explained to Pilate, 'is not of this world. ... My kingdom is not from here' (John 18:36). It is different, first, because at this time it is invisible. His is essentially a spiritual kingship, although no less significant on that account. Invisible as it is to the human eye, it is plain to those with spiritual discernment.

Second, His Kingship is different because He exercises it in His people's innermost being. Those who owe their salvation to Him, and therefore know and love Him, sanctify (or set apart) Christ as Lord in their hearts (1 Peter 3:15). This is not a mere sentimental acknowledgement, but one that influences life and conduct. They delight to live as His subjects, and to obey His laws and teaching. The Lord Jesus lives in His people's hearts as they trust in Him (Ephesians 3:17). He exercises His kingship there by His indwelling Spirit. There is no place in which the Lord Jesus more delights to live than in the hearts of His believing people. It is there by His Spirit that He reveals His glory to His obedient subjects (John 14:21). He makes Himself known to them as He does not to the world at large.

Third, His kingship is different because it is everlasting (Daniel 7:14). To use an expression from the Psalms, the crown upon His Head 'will flourish' (Psalm 132:18). Our Saviour's glories as King will never fade. His kingdom cannot fail. Innumerable crowns have been placed upon the heads of kings, queens, and sovereigns throughout the centuries. Some consisted of laurels and ivy. They have all withered, decayed and perished. Our Saviour's crown never decays. Rather, it blossoms! Other sovereigns have worn crowns of silver and gold. Yet they have tarnished or have been laid aside by death. Not so our Saviour's! Imagine looking at the display of the British Sovereign's Crown jewels in the Tower of London. A guide might comment, 'This crown was worn by Queen Victoria or King George V.' The key word in each case would be the word *was*. We never have to use the past tense of our Saviour's Kingship.

Fourth, our Saviour's Kingship is different because of how He rules us. He exercises His authority over us by His Spirit through His Word. If we think of a King possessing a sceptre, our Lord's sceptre is His Word, the Scriptures. Conscience is important in the Christian's life, but conscience must be educated by the Scriptures and be subject to them. Pastors and teachers are an important provision for the Church in the teaching and preaching of Christ's Word, but we must test and examine all they say by Scripture. Where what they teach is according to it, it is to be accepted, and where contrary to it, rejected. Human reason is a God-given gift, and traditions formed over the years through the acceptance of Christ's truth are invaluable. Nevertheless, both reason and tradition must be tested by Scripture, the sceptre of our King.

Fifth, the Lord Jesus' Kingship is different because He effectively defends us from all our enemies, and ensures our complete protection and safety. He governs everything for His people's good. As John Calvin put it, 'Christ was taken up into heaven, not to enjoy blessed rest at a distance from us, but to govern the world for the salvation of all believers' *(Syn. Gosp. III*, p.393*)*.

Aware of the unceasing activity of our enemy, Satan, He anticipates his every move. Not one of our Saviour's subjects will ever be lost (John 10:28,29; 17:2; 18:9). This does not mean that we are immune from attacks, and may not experience personal defeats. Such are necessary often for our protection, correction and growth in faith. But not one of our King's subjects, given to Him by His Father, will be, or can be, lost.

A Kingship that brings us into tension with the world

Our Lord's Kingship over us brings us sometimes into a state of tension with the world and its authorities. The early Christians endeavoured to be exemplary citizens of the world (as taught by the Lord Jesus—e.g. Matthew 22:18-21). However, when human authorities demanded recognition as great as that of deity (if not deity itself) then they had to draw the line.

Christians suffered persecution and martyrdom when they refused to affirm 'Caesar is Lord' since they reserved that title uniquely for their Saviour and King, according to the Father's will. We know little of such tensions and confrontation in the West, but many experience persecution and death in other parts of the world, as they find their allegiance to the Ascended Lord places them in conflict with the state.

Rulers and civil authorities are always in danger of being intoxicated by power. They may attribute merit to themselves, deify themselves, elevate themselves against God, and even go so far as to offend Him by blasphemy. It is as well to remember, therefore, that the authority God entrusts to human beings is never absolute, but is limited by moral obligations. Civil and other authorities may sometimes choose to listen to the malicious accusations of enemies of the gospel. Some may declare that Christian preaching is a political crime or that Christians are trouble-makers (Acts 17:6; cf. 19:23-27; 24:5). The apostles' answer provides the classic response when temporal authorities command us to stop doing what God has plainly commanded: 'We ought to obey God rather than men' (Acts 5:29).

Usually, however, the fulfilment of our obligations to the state will be an essential part of our Christian testimony that commends both us and the gospel to the powers that be. We are to live in society as God's servants, and by our good citizenship put to silence the ignorant and unjust criticisms of foolish people (1 Peter 2:13-15). The intended norm is that our good behaviour in the world should 'adorn the doctrine of God our Saviour in all things' or, as the NIV translates it, 'make the teaching about God our Saviour attractive' (Titus 2:10).

Governor of the Universe

Besides being His people's King, the Lord Jesus Christ is also the unseen Governor of the universe. Two New Testament statements must influence our thinking. First, He upholds 'all things by the word of His power' (Hebrews 1:3). Creation looks to Him as its strength and stay. Second, 'in Him all things consist' (Colossians 1:17). Whatever else these statements mean, they make clear that Jesus Christ maintains the universe. It owes its coherence to Him. He carries it along to its final goal and destiny. His Ascension is the most political aspect of His work in that it declares Him to be in the place of authority over *everything*. Nothing is excluded from His control. He rules over the world (the cosmos), the powers of darkness and His believing people, the Church (John 16:33; Ephesians 1:19-23).

Right now the world and its rulers in general are in rebellion against our King; but all such rebellion is doomed to fail (Psalm 2:1-6). Probably no human ruler was ever more impressive and grandiose than King Nebuchadnezzar, the Babylonian king, who reigned from 605 to 562 BC. His testimony, following his restoration to sanity after the exercise of God's judgment upon him, was, 'For His dominion is an everlasting dominion, and His kingdom is from generation to generation. All the inhabitants of the earth are reputed as nothing; He does according to His will in the army of heaven and among the inhabitants of the earth. No one can restrain His hand or say to Him: "What have You done?"' (Daniel 4:34,35). Earlier Daniel prophesied of the Messiah's kingdom, 'The God of heaven will set up a kingdom which shall never be destroyed; and the kingdom shall not be left to other people; it shall break in pieces and consume all these kingdoms, and it shall stand forever' (Daniel 2:44).

At this present time the Ascended Jesus, our King, wages war against Satan and his allies (Revelation 17:14). He rules in the midst of His enemies (Psalm 110:2). In spite of all opposition to His invisible Kingdom, He continues to draw men and women to Himself from every tribe and nation

(John 12:32; Revelation 5:9; 7:9). In the places of the world where His cause is most opposed, there is the greatest triumph as He builds His Church and Kingdom—the two are synonymous.

Jesus' judicial reign

The time rapidly approaches for the exercise of our Lord Jesus' rule as Judge. At His return His present sovereignty over all will be displayed (1 Corinthians 15:24-26). The Father has given to the Son all authority to judge (John 5:22). The Father has done this so that all will honour the Son. We will see this purpose on the Day of Judgment in an awesome manner. Kings and queens will stand before Him; presidents, prime ministers and military rulers will lose all the trappings of their puny power before His authority. He is already the Judge, who searches hearts and minds in preparation for that moment of history. He will repay everyone according to his or her deeds (Revelation 2:23). He 'has the sharp, two-edged sword' (Revelation 2:12; cf. 2:16). He has but to speak and His will is done. 'He shall judge among the nations, He shall fill the places with dead bodies, He shall execute the heads of many countries' (Psalm 110:6). He will 'break them with a rod of iron' and He will 'dash them in pieces like a potter's vessel' (Psalm 2:9). The devastating majesty and authority of Jesus Christ can be conveyed now only by restrained pictures. The reality is far beyond our power to anticipate.

The end in view

The Lord Jesus governs the whole universe with one end in view: that God's purposes for the Church may be fulfilled. The word *throne* occurs 62 times in the New Testament, and 47 of those occurrences are in the Book of Revelation. To those who lived at the time John wrote, it looked to all appearances as if Caesar reigned, and that his throne was the final authority. The revelation imparted to John showed that this was not the case, and that there is another and greater throne.

Picture a throne—or a control room—at the centre of the universe. The Lord Jesus governs there in the interests of His people. To this end He stands 'in the midst of the throne' (Revelation 5:6), sharing God the Father's sovereign rule. He holds in His right hand a seven-sealed scroll, generally recognised to represent the book of history (Revelation 5:1). He alone has the ability and authority to open it, and He breaks the seals one by one, as the One who unfolds history, chapter by chapter. As the Lamb, who died for His people upon the Cross, He is uniquely qualified to do this.

A mystery surrounds our Saviour's present rule, since many aspects of it we cannot now understand. So much happens that seems unreasonable, unjust and beyond explanation. Glorious joys go hand in hand often with unspeakable sorrows. At times it does not look as if the Lord Jesus rules in the interests of His people. However, both the Scriptures and our God-given faith assure us that He does. When we reach the end of our journey, we will find, as Job did, that the Lord's plan ends finally in eternal good, no matter what our sufferings and disappointments have been (James 5:11). We will then have ample reason to praise Him. The mysteries of life will be resolved when instead of knowing in part, we shall know fully, just as God knows us now (1 Corinthians 13:12).

The outworking of our Saviour's sovereign purposes in the world may seem like the reverse side of a piece of needlework or tapestry. We may gain some small understanding of what He is doing. but we await the time when the opposite side is completed and shown to us in all its beauty. We are like people looking in from the outside at a building that has stained-glass windows. It is only as we see from the inside, with the benefit of day-light streaming in—as we shall at our Saviour's coming—that we will fully appreciate the glory of what has been achieved during our periods of seeing His purposes all too darkly.

God meanwhile assures us that there is a purpose in history, and that the Lord Jesus and His saving work provide its key. As Paul expressed it, God has 'made known to us the mystery of His will, according to His good pleasure which He purposed in Himself, that in the dispensation of the fullness of the times He might gather together in one all things in Christ, both which are in heaven and which are on earth—in Him' (Ephesians 1:9,10). God has a programme in human history. He will unite all things in His Son, Jesus Christ, things in heaven and things on earth—at the time He has already set. Sin has brought devastating disorder everywhere. In the end, however, everything will be restored to its intended function and unity by being brought back to obedience to our Lord Jesus Christ. We look forward to every creature in heaven and on earth falling before the Lord Jesus as King.

The world, therefore, haphazard as it may seem, is going somewhere. Everything is moving to the great divine end. God's eternal purposes for His Son's Church give meaning to the whole of the human story.

A means to a glorious end

When a Bible statement stands on its own, without similar assertions by which to interpret its meaning, we must always proceed with care. This is especially so regarding the New Testament's description of the end or conclusion of all things as we now understand them.

Paul wrote of the Lord Jesus and His return, 'Then comes the end, when He delivers the kingdom to God the Father, when He puts an end to all rule and all authority and power. ... Now when all things are made subject to Him, then the Son Himself will also be subject to Him who put all things under Him, that God may be all in all' (1 Corinthians 15:24,28). This statement is beyond our present comprehension. We may only guess at what it means. Nevertheless we may be certain of some of its implications. For example, centuries ago Isaiah recognised that his own children were special signs given to him by God. The writer to the Hebrews records our Lord Jesus taking up Isaiah's words: 'Here am I and the children whom God has given Me' (Hebrews 2:13; cf. Isaiah 8:18). The completion of His task of 'bringing many sons to glory' (Hebrews 2:10)—all those chosen in Him before the creation of the world (Ephesians 1:4)—is the sign that His work is done. In His unique position as the Last Adam (1 Corinthians 15:45), the Lord Jesus is able to present all things, and in particular His redeemed people to the Father, and say in effect, 'The whole universe and the children You have given me are now Your obedient servants.' What was lost at the first Adam's rebellion in a spoiled creation and a fallen humanity, will have been gloriously put right and restored by the Last Adam's perfect obedience.

The Lord Jesus' task is to bring to an end all that opposes God's sovereignty. The climax of the plan of salvation will be when He presents to the Father a realm in which His will is supreme and a kingdom filled with obedient sons and daughters. He will have then fulfilled His unique work as the divine King. The Lord Jesus will not cease to rule His people and to be their King, for the eternal kingdom is that of 'Christ and God'

(Ephesians 5:5), that is to say, the Lord Jesus and the Father. The river of the water of life will flow for ever 'from the throne of God and of the Lamb' (Revelation 22:1). But as the Father originated the plan of salvation (e.g. John 3:16), and sent the Son to achieve it, and then sent the Spirit to bring men and women into the good of it, so He will be acknowledged as the source of all things, 'For of Him and through Him and to Him are all things, to whom be glory forever. Amen' (Romans 11:36).

Practical benefits

Understanding these twin truths of our Lord's Kingship of His people and His Governorship of the universe brings great encouragement. When trouble comes, as often it will, we are to turn our eyes to our Ascended Lord. He is in His holy temple and on His heavenly throne (Psalm 11:4). Even as Isaiah viewed events in the world, and in the life of his nation, in a different and proper light when he saw the Lord, the King, 'sitting on a throne, high and lifted up' (Isaiah 6:1), so too will we as we fix our eyes upon the same King Jesus (John 12:41). Calm comes when our hearts rest in His sovereignty. We can be patient in suffering when we are sure of the outcome. We can even have joy in sorrow when we know that nothing is wasted in our King's gracious control of our lives and experiences.

Eyes of faith

A unique and indispensable work of the Holy Spirit is to enable us to see with the eyes of our faith what Isaiah saw. During the ministry of Elisha, successor to the prophet Elijah, Israel was at war with the Arameans. Early one morning Elisha's servant was terrified because he saw that 'there was an army, surrounding the city with horses and chariots. And his servant said to him, "Alas, my master! What shall we do?" So he answered, "Do not fear, for those who are with us are more than those who are with them."' And then Elisha significantly 'prayed, and said, "Lord, I pray, open his eyes that he may see." Then the Lord opened the eyes of the young man, and he saw. And behold, the mountain was full of horses and chariots of fire all around Elisha' (2 Kings 6:15-17).

Our King is always with us, and His resources are constantly available.

We need our eyes opened to see this. William Faber wrote in his hymn entitled, 'The Right must win',

Thrice blest is he to whom is given
the instinct that can tell
that God is on the field when He
is most invisible.

The Lord Jesus ascended as our King to protect us. He ascended as much for our sakes as His own.

Little wonder that Psalm 149 urges, 'Let the children of Zion be joyful in their King', for 'the LORD takes pleasure in His people.' 'Let the saints ... sing aloud on their beds' (Psalm 149:2,4,5). The significance of the reference to 'beds' is not told us, but experience leads me to recognise that it is when I am in bed, awake in the middle of the night, that my fears and anxieties loom largest. At such times Jesus' sovereignty is a pillow upon which to rest.

'Kiss the Son,' Psalm 2 urges (2:12). The kissing of His feet symbolises honouring, confessing, obeying and worshipping Him. In these activities His subjects rejoice. When we realise that we have lost sight of His Kingship, and have failed to live in the light of its truth, we need to reaffirm and rediscover His shout among us.

Preparing a place

No words of Jesus are likely to be more meaningful in the crises of life than those to His disciples on the night He was betrayed. 'Let not your heart be troubled,' He said. 'You believe in God, believe also in Me. In My Father's house are many mansions; if it were not so, I would have told you. I go to prepare a place for you' (John 14:1,2). Understandably perhaps, we tend to reserve the public reading and consideration of this passage for funerals and thanksgiving services at the death of Christian believers. If that is the case, it is regrettable since they have daily relevance to the way in which we think and live.

Paradise regained

Jesus spoke of heaven, and of His preparing a place for His disciples there, in the context of His imminent death, the necessity of which they had not yet fully understood. Jesus' death and our assurance of heaven are vitally connected. He came from heaven to make heaven possible for us. His purpose was to bring many sons (and daughters) to glory (Hebrews 2:10). That great objective, however, could be achieved solely through His atoning death upon the Cross, His supreme act of obedience as the Last Adam. Adam, the father of our human race, tragically disobeyed God in the Garden of Eden. In eating the forbidden fruit of the tree of the knowledge of good and evil, he forfeited the right to eat of the tree of life (Genesis 3:22). He and Eve were then driven out of the Garden of Eden, 'and a flaming sword ... turned every way, to guard the way to the tree of life' (Genesis 3:24). Now, however, those who trust in Jesus Christ are described as having their names written in 'the Book of Life' (Revelation 17:8; 20:12, 15; 21:27) and as belonging to the city of God through which 'a pure river of water of life' freely flows 'proceeding from the throne of God and of the Lamb', with the tree of life on each side of the river in which they may everlastingly share (Revelation 22:1, 2, 14, 17, 19).

Through the Lord Jesus' finished work and our union with Him, we may return and legitimately enjoy the blessings of eternal life from which our first parents, Adam and Eve, were banished. Nowhere was this more dramatically illustrated than at the time of the Crucifixion. A man, whom we know as the penitent thief, had been sentenced to death by the Roman authorities. It was a death he deserved, as he honestly admitted. But death as God's penalty for sin was also what he merited, as we all do. As one of Adam's sons, he too had forfeited paradise. When, however, he put his trust in Jesus, he received the most wonderful promise, a promise made through the power of Jesus' atoning sacrifice, 'Assuredly, I say to you, today you will be with Me in paradise' (Luke 23:43). Through Jesus, who died in his place, as ours, he was forgiven and paradise restored. To use the most profound description the Bible gives of a Christian, he was a man 'in Christ'.

Throughout Jesus' conversation on the night He was betrayed, He indicated and implied the disciples' union with Him. All that He was doing, and was going to do, was for them. They, like us, were to share in His death, for through it they were to receive forgiveness of sins. They, like us, were to participate in His Resurrection, for by it they were to be assured of their acceptance with God through Jesus, and given the promise of physical resurrection. They, like us, were to join Him in His Ascension, for He was going to heaven to prepare a place for them.

The Ascension gloriously reveals what God has planned for His redeemed people before time began. As Paul puts it, God 'raised us up together, and made us sit together in the heavenly places in Christ Jesus, that in the ages to come He might show the exceeding riches of His grace in His kindness toward us in Christ Jesus' (Ephesians 2:6,7). The Lord Jesus became man to share our nature; He returned to heaven that we might share His glory. As now He gives us His grace, so then He will give us the eternal benefits of His love. The whole purpose of His saving work was that we should be with Him beside His Father. 'Father,' He prayed, 'I desire that they also whom You gave Me may be with Me where I am, that they may behold My glory which You have given Me; for You loved Me before the foundation of the world' (John 17:24).

Rightful anticipation

Jesus spoke about the assurance we may have of heaven to encourage the disciples to anticipate with joy and excitement the eternal nature of their union with Him. Stephen, the first recorded Christian martyr, was one who gained strength from this confident expectation. About to be stoned to death because of his testimony to the Lord Jesus, Stephen, 'being full of the Holy Spirit, gazed into heaven and saw the glory of God, and Jesus standing at the right hand of God, and said, "Look! I see the heavens opened and the Son of Man standing at the right hand of God!"' (Acts 7:55, 56). This is the one occasion in the New Testament where it depicts the Lord Jesus as 'standing' at God's right hand. Usually the symbolism is of His sitting, the picture of completion. Jesus' standing expressed His readiness to receive Stephen's soul into His presence and eternal safekeeping the moment he died. He had prepared a place for Stephen in His Father's house, as He does for all believers. Peter wrote of 'the Spirit of glory and of God' resting upon believers in their sufferings (1 Peter 4:14). One of the rich compensations God the Holy Spirit may bring for our encouragement when we suffer painful experiences for the sake of our Saviour, is to make us aware of the glory that is before us. That is particularly appropriate, for the Holy Spirit is described as 'the guarantee of our inheritance', the first instalment of the glory that is to be ours (Ephesians 1:14). No wonder Luke says that as Stephen gave his testimony, immediately before his martyrdom, those who looked intently at him 'saw his face as the face of an angel' (Acts 6:15).

The Bible is reserved in what it reveals about heaven. 'The brakes are on,' as it were. It is careful since heaven is too glorious for words. George MacDonald, a Scottish preacher, was speaking to his son about the wonders of heaven. His little boy interrupted and said, 'It seems too good to be true, Daddy.' A smile spread across MacDonald's whiskered face as he answered back, 'Nay, laddie, it is just *so good* it must be true!' (C.R. Swindoll: *The Grace Awakening*, p. 299). We can only make guesses about some aspects of heaven. If our guesses are not true, something better will be.

When we try to describe to children something more wonderful than they have ever experienced, we often take a picture, or something they know already, and say, 'It is like that, *only bigger and better.*' The Bible similarly resorts to pictures to describe heaven. The variety of descriptions springs from the impossibility of adequately conveying its wonders. Although reserved in what it says, Scripture provides a wealth of images. Heaven is described as a paradise (2 Corinthians 12:2,4). Paradise is a loan word from the Persian language, meaning a garden, or a park with encircling walls, a place of beauty and security. Heaven is thought of as a city, prepared by God for His people (Hebrews 11:16), Mount Zion, the city of the living God, the heavenly Jerusalem (Hebrews 12:22). It is also depicted as a heavenly country, far better than anything known on earth (Hebrews 11:16), a rest (Hebrews 4:9), and the Christian's inheritance (1 Peter 1:4). However, no picture is more meaningful than the Father's house, the one Jesus provided. It is one of the simplest and yet most attractive.

The Father's house

'The house' or 'the home' is the place where others really know us. A home especially reflects a person's character. Heaven is where the Father is perfectly revealed and fully known. It is a place of holiness, love and perfection, for the Father is holy, loving and perfect. It is a place with ample dwellings in which to live (John 14:2). There is room for all who believe on the Lord Jesus Christ for salvation. The Lord of the universe has no problem when it comes to space! The picture is one of intimacy and acceptance. It is not so much that we shall have individual homes, but that inside the one house—the Father's—there is a place for us. All illustrations fail to express fully spiritual truth. But if her Majesty the Queen said to you, 'My palace is in London. You shall have a place there too.' That would not be as wonderful as her saying, 'My palace is in London. You shall live in it too.' The latter is the sense of Jesus' words as He speaks of the Father's house!

Heaven is where Jesus is. It is the sphere of His present life and activity. It is His place of residence where He carries out His special function as our great High Priest. The glory and wonder of heaven is to be with Jesus. The ultimate satisfaction will be seeing Him. Heaven would not be heaven without Him. Those redeemed by Him can wholeheartedly apply to the Lord Jesus the words of Psalm 73:25,26: 'Whom have I in heaven but You? And there is none upon earth that I desire besides You. My flesh and my heart fail; but God is the strength of my heart and my portion for ever.' Because of our wonderful union with the Lord Jesus, and His love for His people, we may also say that heaven will not be fully heaven to Him until all His people, His flock, are safely gathered around Him.

Heaven is a place of glorious family reunion. The disciples were encouraged to anticipate their reunion with their Master. But they were also encouraged, by implication, to look forward to their reunion with one another. He was preparing a place not just for one of them, but for all. Through Him, they had each become one of the Father's children, and when the children are in 'the Father's house', having been apart, they are happily together again, never more to be parted.

None of the disciples knew what was going to happen to them once their Master returned to heaven. All kinds of experiences were before them, as they obeyed their Master's commission to preach the gospel to every creature. Not a few were to face martyrdom. Eventually, however, they were all to be together in the Father's house, to meet again face to face in fellowship with Jesus, their Master, and God the Father, into whose family they had been adopted.

The delight we possess in relationships is an outcome of our being made in the image of God, with the capacity for meaningful friendships. It is not surprising that they are eternally valuable, and that heaven will see us taking them up again, only then without anything ever to spoil them. It will be the most wonderful eternal rendezvous with Jesus in the centre. Alexander Somerville wrote to Robert M'Cheyne, 'Perhaps we may get a lodging near each other in the golden streets of the New Jerusalem' (Smellie: *Robert M. M'Cheyne*, p. 60). The clear implication throughout the Bible is that we shall know one another in heaven. Although our bodies will be changed, our personal identity will continue. Our bodies will be as different as the dull seed is from the beautiful flower (1 Corinthians 15:35-49), the perfect instrument of our new and perfected nature and relationships in God's ever-lasting family.

A sure footing

Our hope—that is to say, our assurance—of heaven is not built upon a false foundation. The Lord Jesus went to great pains to underline this truth to His disciples. Having promised them a home in the Father's house, He said, 'If it were not so, I would have told you' (John 14:2). Jesus said to them, in effect, 'The glory that is before Me is not for Me alone: it is also for you to share. There is not the slightest doubt about it. Can you imagine Me ever deceiving you? I have never deceived you all My time with you, and I am not going to do so now—now that we are going to part.' Living as we do in a world of frequently false expectations, we need to learn to trust what Jesus has said.

Many years ago Edinburgh produced a rascal. His name was John Law, son of a well-to-do Edinburgh goldsmith. John Law had had to escape to France after he had been successful in a duel. In 1719 he began to issue bank-notes in enormous quantities in Paris. They were supposedly supported by gold and silver that remained to be mined in the Mississippi valley. But the problem was that—unknown to the people who trusted in him—this gold and silver had not yet been found! Oh, yes, there were maps circulated in France that showed mines of unimagined wealth, but they were all products of John Law's fertile imagination. Now that is how some people may think of heaven. To them, it is all a matter of promises unsupported by reality. But, in fact, the opposite is the case. All the assurances of heaven in the Bible are backed by the solid gold of God's character, a standard that can never fail.

The best is yet to be

There are other truths about heaven implied in Jesus' conversations with His disciples in the upper room. The first is so obvious that we may almost miss it! *God reserves the best for last!* Jesus' answer to the disciples' doubts, fears and apprehension was to assure them that all such would soon be history, and that unsurpassed joy was to be theirs in the Father's house. Heaven will be perfection. It will be like suddenly becoming adults after having been children. We shall see face to face rather than poor reflections (1 Corinthians 13:11,12). Those features of human life that have caused so much sadness will be removed. There will be no more sorrow, parting, illness, suffering, strife, sin and spoiled relationships. There will be peace without war, knowledge without ignorance, and joy without sorrow. What is more, heaven will be all the more agreeable after the trials and difficulties we may know in this life. It will be more than a sufficient reward for any pain and suffering we may have experienced for the sake of our loyalty to our Saviour (Matthew 5:12). If we could see now the joys of heaven, we would not want to be here, but there!

(Here is not the place to deal with the timing of our entry into heaven, but it may be appropriate to state that the Bible's descriptions of death imply that when Christians die they have an immediate awareness of being with their Saviour and of their eternal well-being. Their spirit—or soul, since the two words are used interchangeably—are consciously in God's presence. Death then is a wonderful deliverance. The soul or spirit finds itself immediately freed from all the weaknesses and disabilities imposed upon it by the human body. At the return of Jesus Christ believers' redeemed spirits will be united with their glorified bodies—see, for example, Philippians 1:21, 23; 3:20, 21).

A new homeland

Second, we are reminded that *we possess a heavenly citizenship*. 'Our citizenship is in heaven,' Paul wrote to the Philippian Christians (Philippians 3:20). Most of us take pride in our human citizenship of the countries to which we belong, but none in the first century were more proud than the Romans since their citizenship brought greatly valued privileges. The reminder had particular relevance to the Philippian Christians because Philippi was a Roman colony. Roman colonies, wherever they might be established in the ancient world, modelled their life not on the country or nation in which they were found, but upon Rome itself. Each was a little 'Rome' among non-Roman populations aiming to be a centre of Roman life. Those who lived in Philippi, situated in northern Greece, although residents of Macedonia, were Roman citizens. Their government was Roman, as were many names of streets and places in Philippi.

Although Christians live in every part of the world, and belong to all its nationalities, our true home is in heaven. While we recognise our duty to obey the laws of our respective governments, we give first allegiance to the laws and commands of our heavenly King. We aim to live in this world now as the citizens of heaven, an endeavour that ought to make us better citizens of the world.

The Lord's Supper is a reminder of our heavenly citizenship because it is essentially a pilgrim's or traveller's meal. We are intended to recall in this way the Lord Jesus and His death for us until He returns, and we enter the full joys of the Father's house. When we lived in London, we had staying with us for a year an American music student, called Priscilla. She showed real homesickness only once. My wife remembered that Thanksgiving Day, a public holiday in the USA, is important to Americans, wherever they may be. To surprise Priscilla we invited another American, one of her friends passing through London, to have a meal with us on that day, doing our best to make it as much like an American Thanksgiving Meal as we could. Besides taking

Priscilla by surprise, it brought tears to her eyes, and made her extremely homesick. She remembered then—as perhaps she had forgotten for a while—that her real home was not in Britain, but in the USA.

The Lord's Supper is designed to make us homesick, nostalgic, for heaven. The original meaning of 'nostalgia' is a longing for home. Captain Cook used it of his sailors who showed all the marks of serious illness. One of Cook's colleagues said at the time that the seafarers 'were now pretty far gone with the longing for home which the physicians have gone so far as to esteem a disease under the name of Nostalgia.' In the Sermon on the Mount, the Lord Jesus said, 'Do not lay up for yourselves treasures on earth, where moth and rust destroy and where thieves break in and steal; but lay up for yourselves treasures in heaven, where neither moth nor rust destroys and where thieves do not break in and steal. For where your treasure is, there your heart will be also' (Matthew 6:19-21). Our hearts and minds are to be set on things above, where our Saviour is (Colossians 3:1-4). Where our treasure is, our thoughts should often be. While we are like exiles from heaven, we should also be like prospective emigrants who are so engrossed in the country to which we are going, asking about it, talking about it, that we are always there in thought and anticipation of our future. Every day we live we are one day nearer heaven.

Life from heaven's perspective

Third, *heaven should be in us before we are in heaven*. That thought is prompted by a comment by Izaak Walton about my favourite Puritan, Richard Sibbes. In a book of Sibbes, preserved in Salisbury Cathedral library, Walton wrote, 'Of this blest man, let this just praise be given, Heaven was in him, before he was in heaven.' One of my grandchildren quizzed me recently about my life, my likes and dislikes, and one of the questions was, 'What would you like to be said of you when you die?' My answer was to quote this delightful comment about Sibbes. If the joy of heaven is being with the Lord Jesus, in the Father's house, the greatest joy on earth is to know the Lord Jesus showing Himself to our souls, and He and the Father making their home with us, as Jesus promises in John 14:21 and 23. While our anticipation of heaven will always be more weak and imperfect than we want, we should be there nevertheless in our hopes, desires and thoughts. The more we meditate on the glory of our Lord Jesus in this world, the more we will want to see it in heaven.

Heaven should often be in our thoughts for two substantial reasons. First, *it puts our present life in proper perspective.* Those whose citizenship extends only to this world, naturally find all their expectations and preoccupations within it. Many live as if material and financial considerations are top of any list. Illness, suffering and the approach of death may seem absolutely catastrophic because they threaten to end all human relationships, hopes and aspirations. When, however, we look at this world in the light of heaven, we recognise that some of the things we so easily become bothered and fussed about are *but things,* and the difficulties only temporary, seen in the light of an eternity in heaven. We recognise too that some of our difficulties of which we would naturally fight shy turn out to be part of our heavenly Father's preparation of us for heaven.

During the Second World War the American President, Franklin Roosevelt, said of Winston Churchill, 'The trouble with Winston is that he enjoyed the old world too much to understand the new' (Sir Robin Day: *Grand Inquisitor*, p. 37). If we fail to let heaven govern our perspective on life, we may find that this old world preoccupies us too much. C. S. Lewis expressed something of the wonder of heaven in his *Narnia* stories with *Aslan* representing our Lord Jesus Christ. One of Lewis' biographers recalls how a member of his family, a little girl, 'after she had read all the Narnia stories, cried bitterly saying, "I don't want to go on living in this world. I want to live in Narnia with Aslan"' (George Sayer: *Jack: C.S. Lewis and his times*, p. 193). Thinking about heaven and the glory that is before us should produce not dissimilar thoughts in us. The more we appreciate what our Lord Jesus does in preparing a place for us in heaven the more we long to be there.

The words of Psalm 84 have even deeper meaning as we apply them to our Father's house. 'How lovely is Your tabernacle, O LORD of hosts! My soul longs, yes, even faints for the courts of the LORD. My heart and my flesh cry out for the living God. ... Blessed are those who dwell in Your house; they will still be praising You. ... For a day in Your courts is better than a thousand. I would rather be a doorkeeper in the house of my God than dwell in the tents of wickedness' (Psalm 84:1,2,4,10).

Psalm 24 is going to receive a new dimension in the future. When our Saviour returns, we will ascend with Him into heaven. For Him it will be a second Ascension, but for us our first. As we approach heaven we will be able to cry, 'Lift up your heads, O you gates! And be lifted up, you everlasting doors! And the King of glory shall come in' (Psalm 24:7). One with 'the LORD strong and mighty', 'the King of glory', there will be no doubt about our entry, and all our enemies will be behind us for ever!

Second, having heaven properly in our thoughts keeps before us *the urgent need of those who as yet do not share our living hope in Jesus Christ*. Probably we are never more aware of the difference being a Christian makes than when we attend the funeral of someone who was not a Christian. Love for our neighbour and our Saviour's compassion for the lost should prompt an ever-increasing concern to share the good news of the One who is the way to the Father and to His house.

A passing remark that Yehudi Menuhin, the great violinist, made about one of his acquaintances struck me forcibly. In New York he was taken by a friend to meet Mr. Henry Goldman, a wealthy man who loved music. The Goldmans lived in an apartment on Fifth Avenue. It was 'far more luxurious' than any Yehudi Menuhin had seen, and 'its walls were covered with Old Masters'. He comments, 'Although he was by then blind, Mr. Goldman would take one round his collection and point to the most minute and wonderful details of each painting; so well did he know them. It was an education, and an experience of unforgettable poignancy, to be shown such riches by a man who saw their glories only with his mind's eye' (Yehudi Menuhin: *Unfinished Journey*, p.129). The glimpses of glory we gain as we know the Lord Jesus Christ should so be 'in our mind's eye' that we live by them and are able to share them with others.

No doubt if we focus more on our Saviour and think and talk more about heaven, and witness by our lives more to its reality, it will provoke others to ask questions about 'a reason for the hope' we have (1 Peter 3:15).

The collect for Ascension Day in *The Alternative Service Book* carefully avoids speculation about the nature of heaven, and the place where our Saviour has gone. Rather, it encourages us to ascend there in heart and mind.

Almighty God, as we believe Your only-begotten Son our Lord Jesus Christ to have ascended into the heavens, so may we also in heart and mind thither ascend and with Him continually dwell; who is alive and reigns with You and the Holy Spirit, one God, now and for ever. Amen.

Waiting

The final picture the Bible presents of our ascended and glorified Lord Jesus is of Him waiting. He awaits His return and final triumph. There is more than one form of waiting. We may wait not knowing what is going to happen, and in such circumstances we feel helpless. That is not the kind of waiting of which we are thinking. We may wait with expectancy and excitement, certain of events that cannot be hindered or forestalled. That is the waiting we have in view.

The Father has said to His Son, 'Sit at My right hand, till I make Your enemies Your footstool' (Psalm 110:1; Acts 2:34, 35), and this He now does (Hebrews 10:13). This promise, and particularly the word 'till', show it was never intended that our Saviour's Ascension should be followed by the immediate suppression of all evil and of all His enemies.

The Bible does not describe in detail the identity of our Lord Jesus Christ's opponents, for they are greater than we can appreciate (Ephesians 6:12). It does mention, however, antichrists (for example, 1 John 2:18) and those who are 'the enemies of the cross of Christ' (Philippians 3:18). His enemies include all who show animosity to His uniqueness, His teaching, His Cross, His kingdom, and His people. He awaits the final surrender of all who propagate false teaching and religion, together with the overthrow of the devil and the supernatural powers of evil (1 Corinthians 15:25).

As our Saviour waits, so too must His people. The *apparent* inactivity of our Saviour is exactly what the Bible leads us to expect. His Ascension has not solved the problem we may have of why God allows evil men to prosper and Satan to do his wicked work. But answers will be forthcoming when the period of waiting is over, and Jesus returns.

The renewal

At this point there are certain basic Scriptures we must take into our thinking. Peter explained, that God will send Jesus Christ 'whom heaven must receive until the times of restoration of all things, which God has spoken by the mouth of all His holy prophets since the world began' (Acts 3:21). In Matthew 19:28 this restoration is called 'the regeneration' or 'the renewal'. Jesus said to His disciples, 'Assuredly I say to you, that in the regeneration, when the Son of Man sits on the throne of His glory, you who have followed Me will also sit on twelve thrones, judging the twelve tribes of Israel.' Peter's words in Acts 3:21 point to the fulfilment of Old Testament prophecy in the establishment of God's kingdom on earth.

The idea of the renewal of all nature at the inauguration of the Messiah's reign is found in Romans 8:18-23 where Paul writes, 'For I consider that the sufferings of this present time are not worthy to be compared with the glory which shall be revealed in us. For the earnest expectation of the creation eagerly waits for the revealing of the sons of God. For the creation was subjected to futility, not willingly, but because of Him who subjected it in hope; because the creation itself also will be delivered from the bondage of corruption into the glorious liberty of the children of God. For we know that the whole creation groans and labours with birth pangs together until now. And not only that, but we also who have the firstfruits of the Spirit, even we ourselves groan within ourselves, eagerly waiting for the adoption, the redemption of our body.'

Years later, in his first letter, after affirming that Jesus 'has gone into heaven and is at the right hand of God, angels and authorities and powers having been made subject to Him' (1 Peter 3:22), Peter writes, 'The end of all things is at hand' (1 Peter 4:7). We seldom read in the New Testament of the Ascension without an accompanying mention of 'the end' or the return of Jesus.

The Judgment

When we considered our Lord Jesus as King and Governor in Chapter Eleven, we referred briefly to His judicial reign. It is especially appropriate to mention it here again. Our Saviour waits for the time when He will exercise this unique prerogative given Him by the Father. Eternal judgment is one of the first or elementary teachings about Christ in which people need to be instructed (Acts 24:25; Hebrews 6:2). In his first public presentation of the gospel in Athens, Paul declared of God, 'He has appointed a day on which He will judge the world in righteousness by the Man whom He has ordained. He has given assurance of this to all by raising Him from the dead' (Acts 17:31). Jesus' Ascension in power is the prelude to His coming in power as the divine Judge. The Lord Jesus implied His future exercise of judgment when He said to the High Priest and those who falsely accused Him, 'Hereafter you will see the Son of Man sitting at the right hand of the Power, and coming on the clouds of heaven' (Matthew 26:64).

Proclaiming the good news of Jesus for the first time to Gentiles, Peter declared that the Lord Jesus has been 'ordained by God to be Judge of the living and the dead' (Acts 10:42). It is the gospel of John that contains most of our Lord's words about His position as the Judge (i.e. John 5:22,27), but that is not exclusively so.

In the other gospels we find a variety of symbolism our Lord used. His coming will be like a stormy day or hurricane when the foundation of men and women's lives will be tested (Matthew 7:24-27). It will be like a time of harvesting when weeds are separated from the wheat (Matthew 13:30,42). It will be like the coming of a bridegroom who refuses to open the door to those he does not recognise (Matthew 25:11ff). It will be like a day of festivities when some are shut out because they are not suitably dressed (Matthew 22:11ff). It will be a day of reckoning, of settling accounts (Luke 12:43ff). It will take the world by surprise as the flood did in the days of Noah (Luke 17:26ff).

Rewards and privileges

The time of the great reversal will follow, when all that is wrong will be put right (Matthew 19:30; 20:16). Believers are to look for their true reward then. For example, Jesus said, 'Blessed are you when they revile and persecute you, and say all kinds of evil against you falsely for My sake. Rejoice and be exceedingly glad, for great is your reward in heaven, for so they persecuted the prophets who were before you' (Matthew 5:11,12).

Nowhere is Jesus' return more graphically described than in Paul's reassuring words to persecuted and tested Christians at Thessalonica. He explains that their patience and faith in all their persecutions and tribulations provide 'manifest evidence of the righteous judgment of God, that you may be counted worthy of the kingdom of God, for which you also suffer; since it is a righteous thing with God to repay with tribulation those who trouble you, and to give you who are troubled rest with us when the Lord Jesus is revealed from heaven with His mighty angels, in flaming fire taking vengeance on those who do not know God, and on those who do not obey the gospel of our Lord Jesus Christ. These shall be punished with everlasting destruction from the presence of the Lord and from the glory of His power, when He comes, in that Day, to be glorified in His saints and to be admired among all those who believe' (2 Thessalonians 1:5-10).

A day of glory for the King's people

For Christian believers there will be breathtaking joy at Jesus' return. They will enter into all the benefits of eternal life, the opposite of eternal destruction. The essence of eternal life is fellowship with God (John 17:3). He will give us the most glorious 'rest' (2 Thessalonians 1:7). Literally, 'rest' can be translated 'let-up'. At this present time there is no 'let-up' in so many demanding aspects of daily life and the spiritual battle in which we are engaged. However, then we will enjoy the glorious rest our Saviour promises and has provided for His people.

We will know close proximity to the Lord Jesus, the full enjoyment of His presence. That delight now is always hindered and limited in some measure by our waywardness. Perfect freedom from sin however will mean unspoiled fellowship with our Saviour. We will walk in the light of His presence (Psalm 89:15).

We will witness and experience the majesty of His power, something from which unbelievers will be totally excluded (2 Thessalonians 1:9). The benefits will be immeasurable. We will be transformed into His likeness (1 John 3:2). Our earthly bodies will 'be conformed to His glorious body' (Philippians 3:21).

We will be something like a mirror reflecting our Lord's glory (2 Thessalonians 1:10). 'As Christ will be admired in His own Person, so His glory, reflected in all His children, will be a subject of admiration to the whole intelligent universe. The saints of God shall be so pure, so bright, such trophies of the Redeemer's power to save that He shall be admired in them' (C. H. Spurgeon). The glory of our Lord Jesus Christ's power and grace will be displayed in us, and with good reason. Everything we have, and will enjoy for ever, comes from Him. Our thanks as His people, throughout all eternity, will be to Him for what He has done for us. How will we be able to thank Him enough for His love in dying for us, His patience in bearing with us, His power in keeping us, and His faithfulness in keeping all His promises?

The breathtaking wonder of it all will overwhelm us. The word 'admired' in 2 Thessalonians 1:10 is used in a sense no longer familiar. It means to be 'wondered at'. Looking at a great work of art, we admire the artist. When the billions of the redeemed stand together, safely gathered into the Father's house, all of them His Son's workmanship, transformed into His likeness, Jesus will be admired and wondered at, to the glory of the Father.

The glory of that day will surpass anything we can imagine. We have all known what it is to have looked forward to a spectacular event like the Royal Tournament in London or the Edinburgh Military Tattoo. At last the time arrived. Our imagination had worked overtime as we thought about it, but when it took place, it was more spectacular than ever imagined. We exclaimed, 'I never thought it would be as wonderful as this!' Our Saviour's return will be like that! We shall be astonished, and lost in wonder, love and praise. Countless multitudes of the redeemed will unite in one universal chorus, singing, 'Worthy is the Lamb who was slain', 'Salvation belongs to our God who sits on the throne, and to the Lamb' (Revelation 5:12; 7:10).

Hymns and songs of every generation of Christians tend to reflect their spiritual preoccupations. Both the return of the Lord Jesus and the implications of the last judgment do not figure much in contemporary Christian worship. We need to remedy this omission since, properly understood, these truths provide necessary stimulus to both holiness and evangelism.

Our responsibility

Until our Saviour's return we are to obey His final commission and guard and cherish the gospel. In terms of the pictures and symbolism of His teaching, we are to demonstrate that the foundation of our faith in Him is well laid by the obedience of faith that it properly produces in our lives (Matthew 7:24-27). Obedience to His Word is of the very essence of our spiritual sonship. We are to use the gift of time and opportunities to serve Him well, so that we will not be ashamed to give Him an account of our stewardship (Luke 12:43ff).

We are to live and behave as members of our Saviour's heavenly kingdom (Revelation 1:6,9). We are to exercise our spiritual priesthood

(Revelation 1:6). We are to bear testimony to Him in the world, at whatever cost (Revelation 1:9), so long as we are faithful to Him (Revelation 2:13). We are to hold fast to our first love, and increase it (Revelation 2:4). We are to safeguard our personal fellowship with Him (Revelation 3:20). We are to persist in all these privileges and duties with 'patience' (Revelation 1:9). Most of all we are to be watchful and ready. His coming is soon (Revelation 3:11), and will be as unexpected as a thief in the night (Revelation 3:3).

Maranatha!

The early Christian greeting was 'Maranatha'. Instead of simply saying, 'Good-bye' as they parted, they reminded one another, 'The Lord is coming!' and they rejoiced. We need to recover this sense of expectancy. The detailed description Christians have wanted to provide of the programme of future events relating to Jesus' coming has sometimes obscured the certainty of His coming and the influence it should have upon daily behaviour. 'What do you think is going to happen in the next few years of history, Mr. Lewis?' Sherwood E. Wirt asked C. S. Lewis in a recorded interview. Lewis' answer was interesting and appropriate: 'I have no way of knowing. My primary field is the past. I travel with my back to the engine, and that makes it difficult when you try to steer. The world might stop in ten minutes; meanwhile, we are to do our duty. The great thing is to be found at one's post as a child of God, living each day as though it were our last, but planning as though our world might last a hundred years' (C.S. Lewis: *Christian Reunion and Other* Essays, edited with a preface by Walter Hooper, p. 93). We are to put our different abilities to work in tasks He has assigned us (Luke 19:13).

One of the purposes of the Lord's Supper is to keep this living hope before us, for we remember our Saviour in the way He established 'till He comes' (1 Corinthians 11:26). When He returns, that meal will be obsolete! When the shout of our King is in our hearts, 'Maranatha' is upon our lips. How loud that shout will be when He comes!

Cause of our failures and secret of our successes

We are spiritually healthy and equipped to do our Lord's work in the world as His shout is among us. To appreciate the significance of Jesus' Ascension and His continuing work is to know the grounds of our confidence for the continuance, endurance and success of His Church, whatever the odds against her may appear to be. To enter into the wonders of His present ministry is to rejoice in His presence and the grace and power always available to His believing people.

The truths we have been considering are spiritual realities by which those born of God's Spirit are to live. Those without spiritual understanding may consider them folly. Those born of the Spirit however find that same Spirit interpreting them and making them meaningful and vital to Christian living and service (1 Corinthians 2:14). As Paul put it, 'For though we walk in the flesh, we do not war according to the flesh. For the weapons of our warfare are not carnal but mighty in God for pulling down strongholds' (2 Corinthians 10:3, 4).

Lessons from Israel

Israel's tragedy was that 'the shout of a King' (Numbers 23:21) was not always with her. Sometimes she had the vocal shout without the inner reality. Sadly, she often forgot the Lord and disobeyed Him. She then began to think as other nations around her did, nations with no 'exodus' experience and saving knowledge of the divine King. Israel, in her foolishness, even became envious of nations that had human kings! Defeat soon followed. *All Israel's failures arose from her neglect of her King*. The same is true for the Church of Jesus Christ. When the King does not have His proper place in the affections of His people, they flounder. They may even reach a point where they supposedly proclaim the gospel, but a gospel without salvation and the Lord Jesus at its heart.

A question of focus

Crucial to the spiritual well-being of God's people are right views of our Lord Jesus Christ. The old maxim remains true:

What think ye of Christ? is the test
To try both your state and your scheme;
You cannot be right in the rest
Unless you think rightly of Him.
(John Newton)

If we lose sight of our Saviour's glory, we lose our sense of wonder at belonging to Him, and our privilege of serving Him.

The first benefit the Lord Jesus gave John exiled on the island of Patmos was a vision of Himself—a vision that showed Him in complete control of John's situation and that of the seven churches of Asia, to whom he was instructed to write. John was impressed by his vision of his Saviour's eyes and feet. His eyes were 'like a flame of fire' and His feet 'like fine brass, as if refined in a furnace' (Revelation 1:14, 15). John recognised that his sight of his Lord's majesty was a glimpse of the LORD Almighty, 'the Alpha and Omega' (Revelation 1:8), 'the First and the Last' (Revelation 1:17), the Amen (Revelation 3:14), the Holy and True One (Revelation 3:7), the Overcomer (Revelation 3:21), the One who was dead and is alive for ever more (Revelation 1:18; 2:8), and the Firstborn from the dead (Revelation 1:5). That vision put all contemporary events into perspective. With such a Lord and Head of the Church, the reasonableness of His call to His servants to be 'overcomers' became crystal clear (Revelation 2:7, 11, 17, 26; 3:5, 12).

The Christian life in every generation continues to involve a battle. The battle is not against the people of the world, but the spirit of the world in its opposition and neglect of God. We also have an enemy within, since our fallen human nature, prone to sin, gives us little rest. Satan too goes about as a roaring lion on the look-out for unwary Christians (1 Peter 5:8). Nevertheless the battle is the *good* fight of the faith (1 Timothy 6:12). It is good because had we not been born again of God's Spirit through faith in the Lord Jesus, we would not be in the battle at all or understand what it is all about.

All Christians may be overcomers as they fix their eyes on the Ascended Lord and look to Him for strength. Psalm 81 exhorts us to make a joyous shout to our King. 'Sing aloud to God our strength; make a joyful shout to the God of Jacob!' (1) The matching of these two statements suggests that to shout aloud to the God of Jacob is to say, in effect, 'You are my strength, not because of what I am, or what I have done, but because of Your grace.'

The whole of the Bible backs up the writer to the Hebrews' appeal, 'Let us run with endurance the race that is set before us, looking unto Jesus, the author and finisher of our faith, who for the joy that was set before Him endured the cross, despising the shame, and has sat down at the right hand of the throne of God. For consider Him who endured such hostility from sinners against Himself, lest you become weary and discouraged in your souls' (Hebrews 12:1-3). Here is the secret of daily inward spiritual renewal. 'Therefore we do not lose heart. Even though our outward man is perishing, yet the inward man is being renewed day by day. For our light affliction, which is but for a moment, is working for us a far more exceeding and eternal weight of glory, while we do not look at the things which are seen, but at the things which are not seen. For the things which are seen are temporary, but the things which are not seen are eternal' (2 Corinthians 4:16-18).

The shout of our King is the assurance of His triumph

Throughout church history there have been periods when the Church has been in decline and her prospects bleak. The Church's extinction has been forecast on innumerable occasions. Nevertheless there has always been a persevering minority whose faith has remained firm. The secret of their perseverance has been their assurance of our Lord Jesus' perpetual triumph, and the certainty of His ultimate victory over all His enemies. In spite of how it sometimes appears, the Lord is winning. He is building His Church, and 'the gates of Hades shall not prevail against it' (Matthew 16:18). We may say with joy, 'Now thanks be to God who always leads us in triumph in Christ, and through us diffuses the fragrance of His knowledge in every place' (2 Corinthians 2:14).

Paul took up a picture familiar to first century readers, although not so well-known to us. Successful Roman generals were given what were known as 'triumphs' when they returned home after their conquests. There were some one hundred triumphs between 220 and 70 BC. To be given a triumph a general had, among other conditions, to have defeated a foreign enemy and to bring home his troops. Titus Vespasian (AD 9-79), for example, had one on his return to Rome. The people of that city shouted 'Triumph' as they rejoiced in what had been achieved.

A triumph was the most impressive manifestation of a conquering general's glory. A Greek historian in Rome said that the person celebrating his triumph brought the actual sight of his achievements before the eyes of his fellow-citizens *(Polybius xxi. 29.1)*. The order in the general's procession was meaningful. Captives and slaves followed him, bearing the spoils of victory. But included in the procession were faithful soldiers who had fought with the general. They shared their general's glory. For them it was enough to be in the triumph.

Bitter and hard experiences took their toll of Paul and his colleagues in the first century. They 'were burdened beyond measure, above strength,' so that they 'despaired even of life' (2 Corinthians 1:8). They were pressed hard in spiritual battles, crushed as flowers and herbs might be so that they were hardly recognisable. However, as a direct result a fragrance issued from their lives. It was not the scent of flowers and herbs but a much more wonderful aroma—the fragrance of the knowledge of Jesus (2 Corinthians 2:14,15). Through their identification with their Master and the troubles over which they triumphed, people witnessed in their lives their Saviour's power, and many were drawn to Him. As the early Christians came to recognise that having endured on Jesus' behalf they would also reign with Him (2 Timothy 2:12), they knew it was enough to be in Jesus' triumph. As Paul appreciated his privilege, it moved him from despair to encouragement and joy.

The shout of our King is the assurance of our Lord Jesus Christ's presence

The Man in glory promises to be always with His people by His Spirit (Matthew 28:20; John 14:18). Psalm 89 declares, 'Blessed are the people who know the joyful sound! They walk, O Lord, in the light of Your countenance.' The NIV translates it, 'Blessed are those who have learned to acclaim you, who walk in the light of your presence' (verse 15). We might paraphrase it, 'Happy are those who declare You to be their King, and who have Your shout in their hearts.'

To properly acclaim our Lord Jesus as King, we must walk in the light of His presence. The shout of our King we have in view is not foolish triumphalism, where we imagine that simply to shout words such as 'Christ is triumphant' or 'the King is with us' work some kind of magic. That is not the nature of faith. We do not bolster our courage by making exaggerated claims. Rather we take our Saviour at His Word, knowing that He is the Truth and that He cannot lie. We count upon His presence because He promises it. We deliberately look to Him, and fix our thoughts on Him, because He is the One who brought our faith into being, and who will bring it to glorious completion (Hebrews 12:2). We show our faith in His presence by living in the light of it. We know Him to be aware of every conversation we have, each decision we make, and all the plans we determine. We aim to live holy and godly lives, wanting to co-operate with Him in His eternal purposes worked out in our contemporary world.

Our Saviour's presence is the secret of our deliverance. He teaches us not to rely upon ourselves, but on Him. He is the source of our spiritual resources. We can do everything to which He calls us through the strength He gives (Philippians 4:13). He is the key to all our victories and successes. One of us on our own with Him is in the majority. He protects and preserves us. Our interests are His interests. There is nothing we need as His people that He cannot be—and is—to us. People talk sometimes about having *something* to shout about. We have *Someone* to shout about!

The control of the Church

We must never forget who is in command of the Church. A constant peril, encouraged by the enemy of souls, is that we should get out of touch with our Head (Colossians 2:19). Satan encourages us to focus instead upon human leadership and methodology.

Those called to leadership in local churches and in groups of associated congregations, must never forget that they are but *under*shepherds of the Chief Shepherd. They lead under His authority, and with the sole purpose of doing His will. They must ensure that they are subservient and submissive to the Church's Head. Those who are led, while they acknowledge spiritual leaders as the Lord Jesus' special gift to them (Ephesians 4:11,12), must ensure that their eyes are focused upon Him rather than upon His chosen instruments.

The blessing to be coveted

The blessing most to be coveted by the Church is the experience of the King's presence. It is the crowning and distinguishing mark of His people. When the Lord said to Moses, 'My Presence will go with you, and I will give you rest', Moses rightly pleaded, 'If Your Presence does not go with us, do not bring us up from here. For how then will it be known that Your people and I have found grace in Your sight, except You go with us? So we shall be separate, Your people and I, from all the people who are upon the face of the earth' (Exodus 33:14-16).

Andrew Bonar, a nineteenth century contemporary and friend of Robert Murray M'Cheyne, wrote in his diary, 'Last Sabbath, our Communion, was full of grace and truth. We thought "the shout of the King was among us"' (Andrew Bonar: *Diary and Letters*, p. 268). Paul coveted the reality of this experience for the Corinthian church, as for all God's people. He yearned that visiting enquirers might be so aware of it that they would spontaneously report, 'God is truly among you!' (1 Corinthians 14:25).

Our Saviour's presence is so vital that we should ask Him to make Himself known in those mysterious and yet definable ways God the Holy Spirit brings about. We should shun all that mars our experience of it, such as unconfessed sin and lack of love for one another. Then we should eagerly anticipate His presence, and look for evidences of it. Such indications are our being spoken to by His Word, our hearts being warmed in love for one another, and our lives being transformed by the King's Word.

Confidence for perseverance

Our confidence for going ahead with God's work day by day, and for engaging in the battles our Lord Jesus calls us to fight, comes from His assured presence with us. Strategies are important, but success does not come from human plans or programmes. Rather it comes from the Lord, and the insights and guidance He provides when we submit ourselves to Him as our King.

The first disciples carefully followed their King's instructions. 'They went out and preached everywhere, the Lord working with them and confirming the word through the accompanying signs' (Mark 16:20). He led them from victory to victory, even though there were innumerable conflicts on the way. Our 'Jerichos' will fall if our King is in command, and we joyfully acknowledge and live under His Kingship (Joshua 5:13-6:27). The Lord Himself is our confidence (Proverbs 3:26).

Joy is one of the acknowledged marks of revival. At such times God's people are made spiritually alive and many unbelievers are added to the Church by the Holy Spirit. 'Will You not revive us again, that Your people may rejoice in You?' the psalmist prays (Psalm 85:6). When revival comes, the shout of a King is among His people. They rejoice in Him and know that nothing is impossible to Him.

While Robert Murray McCheyne was away in Palestine, revival came to the church in Dundee of which he was pastor. When he described in a letter to his father what he found on his return, he referred significantly to his people's singing. 'I have never heard such sweet singing anywhere, so tender and affecting, as if the people felt they were praising a present God' (Alexander Smellie: *Robert Murray McCheyne*, p. 139). When the shout of a King is among His people, they know He is *present*!

Is the shout of our King among us?

That question must be asked. Every local church is made up of individuals and each member is important. The degree to which our King's shout is known in our churches and congregations is vitally related to our personal relationship and obedience to Him.

As individuals we may make *the shout of homage* to our King. We should personally ponder and marvel at His death, Resurrection and Ascension for us. We may say to Him, 'Lord Jesus, You are my Lord and King! All I have and all I am are Yours. I give You back everything—my life, my friendships, my career, my hopes and my all. I want my life to be an expression of my homage to You as my King.' In this way we 'kiss the Son' (Psalm 2:12).

As individuals we may make *the shout of joy at His presence* in our life. Rather than the tragedy of Revelation 3:20, where believers in Laodicea had shut Him out, instead we may daily open our life to Him as to no one else. We may share with Him all our cares, fears, hopes and aspirations. He delights to be the joy of our hearts and the goal of our living. As we delight ourselves in Him, He gives us the desires of our heart—more of Himself (Psalm 37:4)!

As individuals we may make *the shout of faith*. As we survey the tasks He has given us, we may be marked by the optimism of faith. With His help, we may do exploits for Him. We will not be satisfied then with simply maintaining the status quo, but rather we will want to advance. When challenges arise our response will be -

Faith, mighty faith, the promise sees,
And looks to God alone;
Laughs at impossibilities,
And cries, "It shall be done!"

Who knows what God may be graciously pleased to accomplish as together we know the shout of our King!

Question and answer on the Ascension of our Lord Jesus Christ *

Question: What happened when our Lord Jesus Christ ascended to heaven?

Answer: At the Ascension our Lord Jesus Christ returned to the Father and was glorified—the final proof of His completed sacrificial work. He entered then upon His work as priest and king upon the throne—no longer needing to offer atoning sacrifice to God—giving gifts to His Church, and guaranteeing her security and final presence with Him in heaven. He waits now for the time of His final victory.

1: The Ascension:

◆ **A:** The Ascension was a vital link in a chain of fulfilled prophecy, promised both in the Old Testament (Psalm 110:1; Acts 2:32-36) and by our Lord Jesus Christ Himself (Matthew 26:64; John 6:62; 7:33; 14:28; 16:5; 20:17).

◆ **B:** It took place forty days after the Resurrection (Acts 1:3).

◆ **C:** It took place at the Mount of Olives (Luke 24:50; cf. Mark 11:1; Acts 1:12).

◆ **D:** It was witnessed by the apostles, after He had talked with them (Mark 16:19) and then lifted up His hands to bless them (Luke 24:50, 51).

◆ **E:** He was lifted up, and a cloud took Him out of their sight (Acts 1:9).

◆ **F:** The return of the Lord Jesus Christ will be after the pattern of the Ascension (Acts 1:11).

2: What the Ascension was:

◆ **A:** It was an act of God's power (Ephesians 1:19-22).

◆ **B:** It was the necessary completion of our Lord Jesus Christ's death and Resurrection: it proved the full acceptance by God of His single sacrifice for sins for all time (Hebrews 10:12); it marked Him out as Lord, even as the Resurrection marked Him out as the Son of God (Philippians 2:9-11; Acts 2:34-36; cf. Romans 1:4).

◆ **C:** It was the visible ascent of our Lord Jesus Christ, according to His human nature, from earth to heaven (Mark 16:19; 1 Peter 3:22): He was exalted to the place in the universe He had laid aside when He humbled Himself to assume our humanity (Ephesians 4:9,10).

◆ **D:** It marked the Lord Jesus Christ's return to the Father: He went to Him who had sent Him into the world (John 6:62; 7:33; 14:28; 16:5; 20:17).

◆ **E:** It included a further glorification of the human nature of our Lord Jesus Christ: He carried His humanity with Him back to heaven (Hebrews 2:14-18; 4:14-16), and He was highly exalted and glorified in doing so (Acts 2:33; John 7:39; 1 Timothy 3:16), the Father honouring Him with the highest possible honour (Ephesians 1:20-22).

3: The significance of the Ascension:

◆ **A:** God the Father's acceptance of His Son into glory declared decisively and finally His acceptance of Jesus' sacrifice for our sins (Hebrews 1:3; 9:12; 10:11-14).

◆ **B:** The Lord Jesus Christ entered upon His work as a royal priest upon the throne, no longer needing to offer atoning sacrifice to God (Hebrews 7:26, 27; 8:1; 10:21); He entered into heaven to appear now before God on our behalf, representing our cause before the Father (Hebrews 9:24).

◆ **C:** The Lord Jesus Christ, demonstrated by the Ascension to be Lord (Matthew 28:18; Acts 2:36), entered upon His work as King; He is seated at the right hand of God (Matthew 26:64; Acts 2:33; Romans 8:34; Colossians 3:1; Hebrews 1:3; 10:12; 12:2; 1 Peter 3:22), a picture of the unique position the Father has given Him of kingly power and authority over angels, authorities and powers in heaven and on earth (Hebrews 1:13; Daniel 7:13,14; Matthew 26:64; Ephesians 1:21,22; 4:10; Colossians 1:16-18; 1 Peter 3:22).

◆ **D:** The Lord Jesus Christ ascended to receive, as Conqueror, the gifts promised Him for His Church (Ephesians 4:8; Psalm 68:18): He ascended to send forth the Holy Spirit (John 7:39; 16:7; Acts 2:33).

◆ **E:** The Ascension of Christ and the consequent outpouring of the Spirit made possible the numerous gifts of the Spirit which the Church enjoys (Ephesians 4:8,11-13).

◆ **F:** The Lord Jesus Christ ascended to prepare a place for Christians (John 14:2): He is their forerunner, preparing the way for them (Hebrews 6:20; cf. Acts 7:56).

◆ **G:** Christians are already set with the Lord Jesus Christ in heavenly places, for they are made to share by grace, through faith, the Resurrection and Ascension of Christ (Ephesians 2:6): their citizenship is now in heaven and their thoughts and affections should be set there (Philippians 3:20; Colossians 3:1,2).

◆ **H:** In Christ's Ascension Christians have the assurance of a place in heaven (2 Corinthians 4:14; John 14:19) and of their own glorification (Philippians 3:21): God's purpose in giving Christians a share in the Resurrection and Ascension of their Lord is that in the coming ages He might show the immeasurable riches of His grace in kindness toward them in Christ Jesus (John 17:24; Ephesians 2:7).

4. What the Lord Jesus Christ does at God's right hand:

◆ **A:** He lives for ever, holding a permanent priesthood (Revelation 1:18; Hebrews 7:24).

◆ **B:** He rules and protects His Church as its Head (Ephesians 1:22,23), helping the members in need (Hebrews 2:18; 4:15), and giving them power to do great works (John 14:12).

◆ **C:** He governs the universe, and to the end that God's purposes for the Church may be fulfilled (Hebrews 1:3; Ephesians 1:5-14).

◆ **D:** He intercedes for His people on the basis of His completed sacrifice (Romans 8:34): He is our Advocate with the Father (1 John 2:1).

◆ **E:** He waits for the time of His final victory: all His enemies shall be subdued (Psalm 110:1; Acts 2:35; 1 Corinthians 15:24-26; Hebrews 10:13).

◆ **F:** His Ascension in power is the prelude to His coming in power as the divine Judge (Daniel 7:13,14; Matthew 26:64; John 14:28; Acts 10:42; 2 Thessalonians 1:6-10).

*This is taken from *Questions on the Christian Faith Answered from the Bible* by the author. It may be reproduced without permission for the purpose of group Bible studies, etc.

A suggested Order for an Ascension Day Service

Notes:

◆ **1: Readers.** A number of readers (eight) are suggested. This helpfully involves members of the congregation, and they may represent it in terms of age, sex and background. It is suggested that they sit together with the person who is responsible for the conduct of the service, perhaps flanking that individual on either side.

It is imperative that the readers meet beforehand to read aloud their passages, to be encouraged in clarity of diction, and to ensure that they are able to be heard. Rather than the readers announcing where they are reading from in the Bible, it is better that all this information should be contained in a duplicated order of service given to each member of the congregation.

The rehearsal will provide an opportunity of praying together for God's blessing on the service, as will the time before the service as the readers prepare to come out together with the leader when the service is due to begin.

◆ **2: Hymns and songs.** There is such change and diversity in contemporary Christian hymns and songs, it is difficult to know how helpful it is to suggest what should be sung. A combination of the old and the new will be helpful, but whether old or new it is important that whatever is chosen is familiar, so that the concentration can be upon the words, and not the learning of a tune and words.

◆ **3: Merely a suggestion.** If this order is used at all, it does not need to be used in its entirety, or in exactly the way suggested. What is important is that the service should be reverent, meditative, purposeful, joyful and glorifying to God.

◆ **4: The leader's role.** At those points in the service where the members of the congregation are invited to join in audibly with prayers and affirmations, it is important that the leader, or someone else duly appointed, should clearly take the lead so that the congregation has a voice to follow. The leader's suggested words are in **_bold italics_** throughout.

◆ **5: The QUESTION AND ANSWER ON THE ASCENSION OF OUR LORD JESUS CHRIST** in Appendix One may be freely duplicated or copied and given with the Order of Service, if felt helpful.

An Ascension Day Service

Leader: Invitation to worship
'And He led them out as far as Bethany, and He lifted up His hands and blessed them. Now it came to pass, while He blessed them, that He was parted from them and carried up into heaven' (Luke 24:50,51).

'This is the day which the LORD has made; we will rejoice and be glad in it' (Psalm 118:24).

'God has gone up with a shout, the LORD with the sound of a trumpet' (Psalm 47:5).

'Blessed be the God and Father of our Lord Jesus Christ, who has blessed us with every spiritual blessing in the heavenly places in Christ' (Ephesians 1:3).

Let us read in unison the words of Psalm 24:7-10:

'Lift up your heads, O you gates! And be lifted up, you everlasting doors! And the King of glory shall come in. Who is this King of glory? The Lord strong and mighty, the Lord mighty in battle. Lift up your heads, O you gates! And lift them up, you everlasting doors! And the King of glory shall come in. Who is this King of glory? The Lord of hosts, He is the King of glory.'

Hymn

Suggestions:
- The Head that once was crowned with thorns;
- Crown Him with many crowns;
- Christ is made the sure foundation.

Leader: Let us pray
(In some of our traditions we may prefer to pray extemporarily. The following may provide an acceptable alternative or perhaps be helpful in stimulating prayer. If used, the prayer might either be prayed by the leader of the service, or by the worshippers together.)

God the Father, God the Son and God the Holy Spirit, we worship and adore You. We thank You, Father, for the glorious plan of salvation, conceived in Your great love for us, Your sinful and wayward creatures. We thank You, Lord Jesus, that, according to Your Father's will, You willingly gave Yourself for us, to be the atoning sacrifice for our sins. We delight to affirm that You rose from the dead, and took Your body of flesh and bones again in order to ascend to heaven, and there to wait until all Your enemies become Your footstool

We thank You, Holy Spirit, for opening our minds and hearts to understand the plan of salvation and the immeasurable love behind it. We rejoice together in our Saviour's birth, life, death and Resurrection. But today we especially celebrate His Ascension. Illumine our minds by the Scriptures, and cause us to understand more of our Saviour's continuing work for us, so that, responding in praise and thanksgiving as we ought, we may then go out again into the world to fulfil our Saviour's commission. We ask these things in His Name. Amen.

First reader: Let us recall some Old Testament anticipations of the Messiah's ultimate exaltation.

Daniel wrote, *'I was watching in the night visions, and behold, One like the Son of Man, coming with the clouds of heaven! He came to the Ancient of Days, and they brought Him near before Him. Then to Him was given dominion and glory and a kingdom, that all peoples, nations, and languages should serve Him. His dominion is an everlasting dominion, which shall not pass away, and His kingdom the one which shall not be destroyed'* (Daniel 7:13-14).

David wrote, *'The Lord said to my Lord, "Sit at My right hand, till I make Your enemies Your footstool." The Lord shall*

send the rod of Your strength out of Zion. Rule in the midst of Your enemies! Your people shall be volunteers in the day of Your power; in the beauties of holiness, from the womb of the morning, You have the dew of Your youth. The Lord has sworn and will not relent, "You are a priest forever according to the order of Melchizedek"'* (Psalm 110:1-4).

Second reader:

Isaiah wrote, *'For unto us a Child is born, unto us a Son is given; and the government will be upon His shoulder. And His name will be called Wonderful, Counsellor, Mighty God, Everlasting Father, Prince of Peace. Of the increase of His government and peace there will be no end, upon the throne of David and over His kingdom, to order it and establish it with judgment and justice from that time forward, even forever. The zeal of the Lord of hosts will perform this'* (Isaiah 9:6-7).
'Behold, My Servant shall deal prudently, He shall be exalted and extolled and be very high' (Isaiah 52:13).
'Yet it pleased the Lord to bruise Him; He has put Him to grief. When You make His soul an offering for sin, He shall see His seed, He shall prolong His days, and the pleasure of the Lord shall prosper in His hand. He shall see the travail of His

soul, and be satisfied. By His knowledge My righteous Servant shall justify many, for He shall bear their iniquities. Therefore I will divide Him a portion with the great, and He shall divide the spoil with the strong, because He poured out His soul unto death, and He was numbered with the transgressors, and He bore the sin of many, and made intercession for the transgressors' (Isaiah 53:10-12).

Congregation together:
'Worthy is the Lamb who was slain to receive power and wisdom, and strength and honour and glory and blessing!' (Revelation 5:12)

Leader: *Let us glory in the Lamb and in the Cross as we sing:*

Hymn

Suggestions:
- In the Cross of Christ I glory;
- Come, let us join our cheerful songs;
- Meekness and majesty

Third reader: Let us recall from the Acts of the Apostles the day of the Ascension:

'Therefore, when they had come together, they asked Him, saying, "Lord, will You at this time restore the kingdom to Israel?" And He said to them, "It is not for you to know times or seasons which the Father has put in His own authority. But you shall receive power when the Holy Spirit has come upon you; and you shall be witnesses to Me in Jerusalem, and in all Judea and Samaria, and to the end of the earth." Now when He had spoken these things, while they watched, He was taken up, and a cloud received Him out of their sight. And while they looked steadfastly toward heaven as He went up, behold, two men stood by them in white apparel, who also said, "Men of Galilee, why do you stand gazing up into heaven? This same Jesus, who was taken up from you into heaven, will so come in like manner as you saw Him go into heaven." Then they returned to Jerusalem from the mount called Olivet, which is near Jerusalem, a Sabbath day's journey' (Acts 1: 6-12).*

Fourth reader: Let us ponder the significance of the Lord Jesus ascending to sit down at the right hand of God:

'God, who at various times and in various ways spoke in time past to the fathers by the prophets, has in these last days spoken to us by His Son, whom He has appointed heir of all things, through whom also He made the worlds; who being the brightness of His glory and the express image of His person, and upholding all things by the word of His

power, when He had by Himself purged our sins, sat down at the right hand of the Majesty on high' (Hebrews 1:1-3). 'For such a High Priest was fitting for us … who does not need daily, as those high priests, to offer up sacrifices, first for His own sins and then for the people's, for this He did once for all when He offered up Himself' (Hebrews 7:26, 27).

'Now this is the main point of the things we are saying: We have such a High Priest, who is seated at the right hand of the throne of the Majesty in the heavens' (Hebrews 8:1).

Fifth reader: Let us remember the glory of our Ascended Lord.

John testified, 'I, John, both your brother and companion in tribulation, and kingdom and patience of Jesus Christ, was on the island that is called Patmos for the word of God and for the testimony of Jesus Christ. I was in the Spirit on the Lord's Day, and I heard behind me a loud voice, as of a trumpet, saying, "I am the Alpha and the Omega, the First and the Last," and, "What you see, write in a book and send it to the seven churches which are in Asia: to Ephesus, to Smyrna, to Pergamos, to Thyatira, to Sardis, to Philadelphia, and to Laodicea." Then I turned to see the voice that spoke with me. And having turned I saw seven golden lampstands, and in the midst of the seven lampstands One like the Son of Man, clothed with a garment down to the feet and girded about the chest with a golden band. His head and hair were white like wool, as white as snow, and His eyes like a flame of fire; His feet were like fine brass, as if refined in a furnace, and His voice as the sound of many waters; He had in His right hand seven stars, out of His mouth went a sharp two-edged sword, and His countenance was like the sun shining in its strength. And when I saw Him, I fell at His feet as dead. But He laid His right hand on me, saying to me, "Do not be afraid; I am the First and the Last. I am He who lives, and was dead, and behold, I am alive forevermore. Amen. And I have the keys of Hades and of Death"' (Revelation 1:9-18).

Paul wrote, 'He is before all things, and in him all things consist' (Colossians 1:17).

The members of the congregation stand together to declare:

Lord Jesus, King of glory, the delight of the Father, and the true joy of our hearts, we are privileged to acknowledge Your glory. You are the Governor of the universe: what You open no-one can shut, and what You shut no-one can open. We declare You to be our King.

The shout of a King **147**

Your kingdom is not of this world, but from another place, from which we look for You to come. Meanwhile we desire to set You apart in our hearts as Lord. Amen.

Hymn

Suggestions:
◆ Crown Him with many crowns;
◆ At Your feet we fall, mighty risen Lord

Leader to pray:
Lord Jesus, from the fulness of Your grace we have all received one blessing after another. You are able to save completely those who come to God through You; You always live to intercede for us. We marvel and rejoice that You have taken our humanity with You to heaven. In our moments of desperation, whether through weakness, suffering or difficulty, help us to fix our eyes upon You, and to find in You our comfort and strength.

Congregation to say together, after the Leader says,

Let us rejoice in our great High Priest's care of us as we say together,

*Though now ascended up on high,
He bends on earth a brother's eye;*

*Partaker of the human name,
He knows the frailty of our frame.*

*Our fellow-sufferer yet retains
A fellow-feeling of our pains,
And still remembers in the skies
His tears, His agonies and cries.*

*In every pang that rends the heart,
The Man of Sorrows had a part;
He sympathises with our grief,
And to the sufferer sends relief.*

(Scottish Paraphrases: Michael Bruce, 1746-67)

Sixth reader: The Lord Jesus has given us the Holy Spirit and with Him spiritual gifts:

*The Lord Jesus promised, 'And I will pray the Father, and He will give you another Helper, that He may abide with you forever—even the Spirit of truth, whom the world cannot receive, because it neither sees Him nor knows Him; but you know Him, for He dwells with you and will be in you. I will not leave you orphans; I will come to you' (John 14:16-18).
Paul explained, '"When He ascended on high, He led captivity captive, and gave gifts to men." ... And He Himself gave some to be apostles, some prophets, some evangelists, and some pastors and teachers, for the equipping of the saints for the work of ministry, for the edifying*

of the body of Christ, till we all come to the unity of the faith and the knowledge of the Son of God, to a perfect man, to the measure of the stature of the fullness of Christ' (Ephesians 4:8, 11-13).

Leader to pray:
Lord Jesus, thank You for the precious gift of God the Holy Spirit to be another Counsellor, and for not leaving us as orphans. Thank You for the gifts He brings to the Church. Help us neither to grieve nor quench Him, and to exercise every gift for the glory of Your Name and the good of others.

Seventh reader:

Let us remember with joy that our Lord Jesus prepares a place for us. He says to us, as to His first disciples, 'Let not your heart be troubled; you believe in God, believe also in Me. In my Father's house are many mansions; if it were not so, I would have told you. I go to prepare a place for you. And if I go and prepare a place for you, I will come again and receive you to Myself; that where I am, there you may be also' (John 14:1-3). Our Saviour prayed for us as well as the first disciples when He said, 'Father, I desire that they also whom You gave Me may be with Me where I am, that they

may behold My glory which You have given Me; for You loved Me before the foundation of the world' (John 17:24).

Congregation to pray in unison, with the Leader taking the lead:

Our Heavenly Father, You have seated us already in the heavenly realms in our Lord Jesus, so that in the coming ages You might show the incomparable riches of Your grace expressed in Your kindness to us in Him. We rejoice and thank You for all that You have prepared for those who love You.

Lord Jesus Christ, thank You for Your desire that we should be where You are, and see Your glory. As You prepare a place for us in heaven, prepare us now for that place. Since our citizenship is in heaven, grant that our hearts and minds may be set more and more on things above where You are.

Holy Spirit, we thank You for Your presence in our lives, a benefit that assures us of the reality of all that is promised us. So work in us that our lives may reveal our heavenly citizenship and show how attractive the gospel of Christ is. Lead us day by day in the way everlasting. Amen

Hymn

Suggestions:
◆ I know that my Redeemer lives;

♦ Jesus is King and I will extol Him;
♦ Glory be to God the Father

Brief address (10 to 15 minutes)
Ideally, a meditation on an aspect of our Lord's Ascension and continuing work, perhaps opening up a simple statement from one of the Scriptures already read.

Examples

Luke 24:51, focussing upon the truth that the last picture the disciples had of Jesus was of His blessing them, and perhaps linking this with John 1:16.

Isaiah 52:13, especially pondering how we see the three promised steps fulfilled in our Lord's Ascension.

Eighth reader: Let us anticipate with joy the return of our Lord Jesus Christ:

'Behold, He is coming with clouds, and every eye will see Him, and they also who pierced Him. And all the tribes of the earth will mourn because of Him. Even so, Amen' (Revelation 1:7).
'And behold, I am coming quickly and My reward is with me, to give to every one according to his works. I am the Alpha and the Omega, the Beginning and the End, the First and the Last' (Revelation 22:12-13).

Congregation together: *'Amen. Even so, come, Lord Jesus!'*

For congregations familiar with the Apostles' Creed, it would be appropriate to join together in this declaration of Christian faith at this point.

The Apostles' Creed

I believe in God, the Father almighty,
creator of heaven and earth.
I believe in Jesus Christ, his only Son, our Lord.
He was conceived by the power of the Holy Spirit,
and born of the Virgin Mary.
He suffered under Pontius Pilate,
was crucified, died, and was buried.
He descended to the dead.
On the third day he rose again.
He ascended into heaven,
and is seated at the right hand of the Father.
He will come again to judge the living and the dead.
I believe in the Holy Spirit,
the holy catholic Church,
the communion of saints,
the forgiveness of sins,
the resurrection of the body,
and the life everlasting. Amen.

(The text of the Apostles' Creed is that of the *International Consultation on English Texts* [ICET], used in *Hymns for Today's Church.)*

Hymn

Suggestions:
- Lo, He comes;
- Look ye saints;
- Rejoice the Lord is King;
- When the Lord in glory comes.

Leader: Benediction

May the Lord bless us and keep us; may the Lord make His face shine upon us and be gracious to us; may the Lord lift up His countenance upon us and give us His peace. May the people of God be glad in their King. Amen